CAMBRIDGE LIBRARY COLLECTION
Books of enduring scholarly value

Music

The systematic academic study of music gave rise to works of description, analysis and criticism, by composers and performers, philosophers and anthropologists, historians and teachers, and by a new kind of scholar - the musicologist. This series makes available a range of significant works encompassing all aspects of the developing discipline.

The Philosophy of Music

Joseph Goddard (1833–1910) was a philosopher and historian of the music of the late eighteenth and early nineteenth centuries. In this collection of essays, first published in 1862, he argues that 'music is the most original and perfect offspring of the human mind'. He first demonstrates this by comparing music with the other fine arts in their expression of emotion, and shows music to have its roots in language, as both depend on principles of rhythm, tone and phrase. He then illustrates how these elements can express the full spectrum of human thought and morality, including truth, faith, imagination and intellect, and asserts that they stand above all other art forms in their ability to do so. Concluding with an analysis of how the laws of life, nature and the supernatural are manifested in music, this judicious work remains important in the fields of music philosophy and theory.

Cambridge University Press has long been a pioneer in the reissuing of out-of-print titles from its own backlist, producing digital reprints of books that are still sought after by scholars and students but could not be reprinted economically using traditional technology. The Cambridge Library Collection extends this activity to a wider range of books which are still of importance to researchers and professionals, either for the source material they contain, or as landmarks in the history of their academic discipline.

Drawing from the world-renowned collections in the Cambridge University Library, and guided by the advice of experts in each subject area, Cambridge University Press is using state-of-the-art scanning machines in its own Printing House to capture the content of each book selected for inclusion. The files are processed to give a consistently clear, crisp image, and the books finished to the high quality standard for which the Press is recognised around the world. The latest print-on-demand technology ensures that the books will remain available indefinitely, and that orders for single or multiple copies can quickly be supplied.

The Cambridge Library Collection will bring back to life books of enduring scholarly value (including out-of-copyright works originally issued by other publishers) across a wide range of disciplines in the humanities and social sciences and in science and technology.

The Philosophy of Music

A Series of Essays

JOSEPH GODDARD

CAMBRIDGE UNIVERSITY PRESS

Cambridge, New York, Melbourne, Madrid, Cape Town,
Singapore, São Paolo, Delhi, Tokyo, Mexico City

Published in the United States of America by Cambridge University Press, New York

www.cambridge.org
Information on this title: www.cambridge.org/9781108038621

© in this compilation Cambridge University Press 2011

This edition first published 1862
This digitally printed version 2011

ISBN 978-1-108-03862-1 Paperback

This book reproduces the text of the original edition. The content and language reflect the beliefs, practices and terminology of their time, and have not been updated.

Cambridge University Press wishes to make clear that the book, unless originally published by Cambridge, is not being republished by, in association or collaboration with, or with the endorsement or approval of, the original publisher or its successors in title.

THE
PHILOSOPHY OF MUSIC.

THE PHILOSOPHY OF MUSIC:

𝔄 Series of Essays,

ENTITLED, RESPECTIVELY,

THE RELATIONSHIP OF MUSIC TO THE OTHER FINE ARTS;
THE MORAL THEORY OF MUSIC;
AND
THE LAWS OF LIFE IN ART.

BY

JOSEPH GODDARD.

"Then stirs the feeling infinite . .
 . . . . . it is a tone
The soul and source of Music, which makes known
Eternal Harmony, and sheds a charm
Like to the fabled Cytherea's zone,
Binding all things with beauty."
                                      Byron.

LONDON:
BOOSEY & SONS, HOLLES STREET.
1862.
[*The right of translation is reserved.*]

TO

MUSICIANS

THIS BOOK

IS RESPECTFULLY INSCRIBED

BY

THE AUTHOR.

CONTENTS.

	PAGE
INTRODUCTORY REMARKS	1
THE RELATIONSHIP OF MUSIC TO THE OTHER FINE ARTS	15
THE MORAL THEORY OF MUSIC	41
THE LAWS OF LIFE IN ART	145

LIST OF SUBSCRIBERS.

	No. of Copies
M. MEYERBEER	2
M. W. BALFE, Esq.	1
JULES BENEDICT, Esq.	1
Madame JENNY LIND GOLDSCHMIDT	1
HERR OTTO GOLDSCHMIDT	1
Miss ARABELLA GODDARD	1
Mrs. ANDERSON (Pianiste to Her Majesty, and Musical Instructress to H.R.H. the Princess of Prussia, H.R.H. the Princess Alice, H R.H. the Princess Helena, and H.R.H. the Princess Louisa)	1
J. W. DAVISON, Esq.	1
G. F. ANDERSON, Esq., Director of H. M. Private Band	1
C. E. MUDIE, Esq.	1
EDWARD JAMES, Esq., Q.C.	1
AUGUSTINE SARGOOD, Esq.	1
J. L. HATTON, Esq.	1
J. F. DUGGAN, Esq.	1
E. F. RIMBAULT, Esq., LL.D., F.S.A.	1
J. ELLA, Esq.	1
C. STEGGALL, Esq., (Mus. D. Cantab)	1
WILLIAM CHAPPELL, Esq., F.S.A.	1
C. SALAMAN, Esq.	1
The Musical Union Institute, Hanover Square	1
The Musical Society of London, Baker Street	1
Messrs. BOOSEY & SONS	12
Messrs. ADDISON & Co.	12

LIST OF SUBSCRIBERS.

	No. of Copies.
Brinley Richards, Esq.	1
W. T. Best, Esq.	1
Cipriani Potter, Esq.	1
Sir George Smart	1
Adolphus Ferrari, Esq.	1
Sig. Belletti	1
Desmond Ryan, Esq.	1
Frank Mori, Esq.	1
G. W. Martin Esq.	1
W. G. Cousins, Esq.	1
Charles Gardner, Esq.	1
W. Dorrell, Esq.	1
Lindsay Sloper, Esq.	1
J. Williams, Esq., H. M. Private Band	1
F. B. Jewson, Esq.	1
J. B. Chatterton, Esq.	1
T. Murby, Esq.	1
Messrs. S. J. & C. E. Stephens	1
W. H. Eayres, Esq.	1
J. Thomas, Esq.	1
J. Lidel, Esq.	1
F. Kinkee, Esq.	1
J. S. Ryall, Esq., Dublin	1
J. Smyth, Esq., B. M., Royal Artillery, Woolwich	1
J. Clafton, Esq., Hythe	1
Llewellen Llwyvo, Esq., Denbigh	1
C. C. Riley, Esq., N. J., America	2
J. W. Spark, Esq., Organist, Town Hall, Leeds	1
W. G. Stockley, Conductor Birmingham Choral Society	1
W. S. Burnett, Esq., Belfast	1
C. J. Hargitt, Esq., Conductor Edinburgh Choral Union	1
J. C. Sherwin, Esq., Burslem	1
Julien Adams, Esq., Glasgow	1
H. E. Ford, Esq., Carlisle	1
R. T. Wilson, Esq., Heversham	1

LIST OF SUBSCRIBERS.

	No. of Copies.
W. C. AINLEY, Esq., Huddersfield	1
W. HENSHAW, Esq., Durham	1
CHARLES BRAID, Esq.	1
JOHN FULCHER, Esq.	1
Dr. ROGERS	1
Miss ANNIE COX	1
The Kingsland Book Society	1
ERASTUS ROGERS, Esq.	1
L. CECCONI, Esq.	1
CARL KLINDWORTH, Esq.	1
H. FROEHNORT, Esq., B.M., 2nd Life Guards	1
C. MANDEL, Esq.	1
D. SMITH, Esq., Exeter	1
JAMES MORRISON, Esq., Glasgow	1
T. BARBER MIGHT, Esq., Dublin	1
HENRY FARMER, Esq., Nottingham	1
EDWARD SEWELL, Esq., Leeds	1
— CATER, Esq., Pall Mall	1
J. P. JEWSON, Esq., Stockton	1
W. ALPHONSE LEGGATT, Esq., Northumberland	1
T. REES EVANS, Esq., Berwick-on-Tweed	1
Messrs. EWER and Co.	1
Messrs. ASHDOWN and PARRY	1
Messrs. DUFF and HODGSON	1
A. CHAPELL, Esq.	1
C. LONSDALE, Esq.	1
R. OLLIVIER, Esq.	1
J. MORTON, Esq.	1
R. REEVES, Esq.	1
Miss MARY H. RICHARDSON	1
J. ROSS, Esq.	1
M. PHILIPPE C. E. SPECHT GRYP, (employé 1re classe de sa Majesté, le Roi des Pays Bas, Aux Indes)	1
Miss SPECHT GRYP	1
S. DE WYLDE, Esq.	1

LIST OF SUBSCRIBERS.

	No. of Copies.
— Loman, Esq.	2
J. Manning, Esq., L.S.A., M.R.C.S.	2
H. Fowler, Esq.	1
Mrs. Ibach	1
Mrs. Rodocanachi	1
S. W. Cantrill, Esq.	1
H. Goddard, Esq.	1
W. Goddard, Esq.	1
W. Moore, Esq.	1
James Beckingham, Esq.	1

PREFACE.

Music is the most original and perfect offspring of the human mind. In the production of this effect, man is permitted to consummate an act approaching nearer to that of creation than in any other of his efforts. If we regard the Art of Painting, we perceive it has a spirit and a form; the spirit is breathed into it by man, but the form is borrowed in completeness from Nature. In Poetry, again, the spirit is inspired by man, but the form,— the imagery, the action, the objects, events, and characters—is copied from the outer world. In the case of Music, on the other hand, man not only bestows the soul, but, to all appearances, the form also; for where in Nature do we find a musical effect bearing anything like a close resemblance to the effects of the Art? —and where do we find *any* effect more beautiful and unique?

Music, again, as a medium for kindling or

expressing emotion, is the most mighty of all the effects of Art; it is that effect most inherently tinged with what we imagine are the attributes of the spiritual world—beauty etheral, yet most real; it is an effect most potent and original in its influence, yet most inscrutable as to the moral constitution of that influence.

These are the general considerations which in the first place impelled me to endeavour to investigate philosophically the nature of Music, moral and material; and the result of this endeavour constitutes the present work. The field I have thus presumed to explore, though, without doubt, pregnant with light and the new riches of truth, is still so vast, and occupies a sphere into which it is so difficult to carry the ordinary reasoning faculties, that it would be a bold thing for anyone to assume he had exhausted it.

Of so much of this task as may be executed in the following pages, I would remark,—it is possible the matter eliminated may be more worthy of attention than the manner in which it is presented. I would also hint to the reader, not to expect to derive from this work much entertainment; the undertaking it clothes is literally a *labour*, it assumes in a great measure the form of argument, and appeals in a considerable degree to the working faculties of the mind.

In concluding this preface, I beg to express my deep thanks to the Subscribers to the work, and others, who by their generous encouragement and kind support have promoted considerably its publication. Whilst doing this I am still sensible that the aid thus accorded me is bestowed mainly from sympathy for the Art, and from a wish to see tha great desideratum in connection with Music supplied—its intellectual bearings explored—its connection with the higher truths of the world pointed out. I hope earnestly that in some respects the book may be of service to the cause.

J. G.

67a, St. Paul's Road,
Camden Square.

INTRODUCTORY REMARKS.

It must be matter of observation that the practice of commenting upon art has now become a field of independent mental exertion, it having of late years been shown that, in the investigation of works of art, faculties and gifts of mind have been elicited as great and original as those which produced the art itself.

The reason of this is apparent in the consideration that amongst the votaries of the arts there are always some in whom susceptibility to impression is greater than the faculty of demonstration. In these the artistic energy vents itself in adding its fire to ideas already formed and inspired; in imparting a second soul to an object of art, by means of some other medium of expression. It may be language. Thus their minds are driven into the *recesses* of the object of art they contemplate. Thus the artistic impulse is brought to bear upon Art itself, and thus the above object comes out from this process still further spiritualised.

If I were to define art generally, I should say—" it is that outer undulation of the human mind which embraces all the inner circles of thought, and mirrors in a spiritual medium the image of the common shore of life."

But defining its process seriatim, I should say it is preceded by a distinct emotion of admiration, created through the influence of some external object of beauty, or by an indefinite rapture of feeling aroused by the general action of outward nature, upon the sense and intelligence of man. It arises in the tendency this condition of feeling exerts to push the pent ardour, amassed in the receptive channels of the mind, outwardly, through the demonstrative faculties of the nature; to employ the outward senses; to wreak itself upon expression.

In consummating this expression, it involves the action of that remarkable tendency prevailing in the human breast whenever charged with an emotion partaking of the character of admiration,—to reproduce, to conjure up again and again the natural influence of that feeling. Thus the painter reproduces upon canvass the fair aspect of nature that impresses him—thus the lover conjures up, in poetic rhapsody, the charms which excite his admiration.

Now, this reproduction of the external influence of emotion constitutes Art. But it must be remarked that the impulse of the breast, thus resulting in art, is reflex in its action. For the representation of an outward incentive of feeling not only in its production employs the demonstrative faculties—not only constitutes the expression of an emotion, but in its effects re-acts upon the receptive faculties, and also perpetuates the emotion.

Thus Art is the embodying an inward idea of beauty, by repeating· in ideal form the external influence of that idea, and the expressing and perpetuating an emotion of admiration in the production, and by the effect of this embodiment. This is Art, and this is the operation of a great principle of the human mind, by means of which it may be said to multiply its offspring, to perpetuate the existence of its own emotions.

From this principle the whole phenomenon of art is developed, and by its aid can be accounted for. The distinction in character, for instance, between a natural influence and the same influence reproduced in the aspect of art, may be thus explained. The mind, in reproducing the object that elicited its admiration, recreates it in the light of that admiration, with those attributes of charm only visible in its original aspect, through the medium of æsthetic taste and poetic meditation, in its artistic form, shining outwardly and apparent to ordinary contemplation. Thus it may bear its original shape, but its soul is no longer hidden, its beauty shines outwardly. It may reappear in bodily form, but its expression is spiritual.

Through these few remarks upon the general constitution of art, it will be understood how the attentive and intelligent observer of *art* may gain a deep insight into *truth;* how, through the *effect* of art, he may behold the *spirit* of nature; how it has been the destiny of many earnest writers upon art to attain to this comprehensive vision; to wield the Ithuriel spear of art as an instrument of moral application.

Poetry, painting, sculpture, and architecture, have, in several instances, led their commentators and recorders to totally new and original eminences of mental observation; and thus to these arts the human mind in general is greatly indebted for the discovery of truths of deep import, and beauties of all-pervading influence. On the other hand, Music, of all the arts, has hitherto been the least serviceable in guiding the mind on its path of moral inquiry. The reason of this may be that, of all the arts, music is that which, in its own conquest and acquisition, absorbs more undividedly the whole attention, monopolises more completely the varied faculties, claims in a greater degree the continued experience of man, and thus reduces the function of its votaries solely to the illustration and interpretation of its simple effect.

There may also exist another reason, which is revealed in the consideration, that music, with regard to other ministrations of art, deals the least with the palpable forms and influences of nature and is the only one without the faculty of representing them in their natural aspect. Consequently, in tracing its influence, in wandering amongst its array of expositions, we meet with no effect common to other branches of moral demonstration, and with no object of external human interest. And thus the large sphere of *suggestiveness* which these influences possess is lost in the contemplation of music. Thus the mind in the exploration of music does not arrive at *new starting points of thought*, but traversing the ethereal stream of sound, glides continuously on its emotional course, undiverted into new channels by the external features of nature.

In the analysis also of musical effect we are searching into that which we cannot grasp, cannot see, and can only feel. Thus, in inquiring into an effect we are analysing an emotion; whereas in the analysis of other effects of art, the mind is brought into contact with a material influence. In music it is mind acting upon mind. In the other arts, mind acting upon matter. In the case of music the intellect works inwardly. In that of the other arts, outwardly. And thus the result is that in commenting upon musical effect, the mind is lost in its own mazes and checked in its progress. Thus its lucubrations in this direction are mostly of a metaphysical character; and meeting with so little support and light from without, the borrowed light of fancy, and vague imagination is so often visible upon them.

In the following pages, however, an attempt is made to push the fragile skiff of thought along this subtle current; and by aid of the compass of known truth, the rudder of argument, and other mental means for obtaining steadiness and straight progress, to gather reliable and practical information upon the nature and meaning of musical effect in the mind; to probe to its source this mystic Nile of tone, and to establish thereupon a few firm positions for the human intellect to affix its standard.

And as the deeper the voyager of discovery

penetrates into the recesses of nature, the greater becomes his knowledge of the laws of his own being, so does the mind in exploring its empire inevitably refract light upon itself; so may we in our present path of research gather new truth for the mind, as well as in casting the light of conquest upon our subject, still further develop its resources.

When we pause in admiration of a flower, the reason is not only lulled by the absorbing influence of beauty upon the senses, and its subtle property of reaching the finer perceptions, without arousing the mind to conscious action; but the activity of the intellect is further superseded through the consciousness we possess of the origin and function of the flower in question. We do not regard this effect as the poet the stars, which he describes as " a beauty *and a mystery.*" On the other hand we are all the while aware that the flower is a natural and necessary feature in the development of the plant whereon it grows. Though there may be in this object much food for reflection, there is still therein nothing, as in the case just alluded to, which strongly arouses the mental activity simultaneously as it invokes the admiration. Now this is the distinction at the outset between the state of the mind in contemplating the effects of all other species of art, and that which it assumes when wrought upon by the influence of music.

Here is a strangely beautiful phenomenon. But what is it? Is it " bright effluence of bright essence increate," or where is the connection between it and the world's more palpable and functional influences; as the flower and its subtle odour that floats like sound through the air is threaded to the rest of nature by the fine fibres of the plant?

Now, in the course of the arguments pursued in the essay termed " The Moral Theory of Music," it is shown that music is *the flower of human speech*.

That where language in its burden partakes mostly of passion and emotion, where it has passed into a totally different principle of demonstration to that of symbolical suggestion; where it attains its highest expression, its most rarefied form. In the fervent " tone," the nervous "inflection," the striking " emphasis," and the suggestive " pause"— that here is to be found *the beginning of music*. That here in embryo exist its different elements, forms, and styles. That it is developed from the ordinary materials of language, as the blossom from the substance of the shrub; that it retains the finer attributes of speech, as the flower still possesses in its roseate petals, the beautified likeness of the green leaves; and that it loses the mixed and dull sound of ordinary language, and wholly assumes the vesture of melody, as the flower relinquishes the opaque and neutral tints of the plant, and beams totally in the dazzling raiment of colour.

In the essay termed "The Relationship of Music to the other Fine Arts," that relationship, so often entered into by writers upon art, is precisely determined. It is shown in this essay, that whereas all other branches of fine art express and convey the sentiment of its conceiver by reproducing, in æsthetic medium, the influence of that sentiment in its natural form, (thus establishing in the case of the contemplator a similar relationship to the original influence as existed in that of the conceiver), as in painting, poetry, and the drama, Music does not; but imparts *the sentiment direct.* That it does not copy the natural features or form, but only the spirit, of any influence. That music is itself *emotion's natural form*. And that in cases where emotion, conducted into the breast through the medium of music, suggests, as emotion often does, its correlative pictures to the mind; the process thus occurring, through the influence of music, is exactly the *inverse* of that which ensues through other æsthetic influence. All other arts conveying the natural incentive of emotion first, and then the emotion. Music imparting first the emotion, and the incentive subsequently.

In closing these preliminary observations, it may be remarked, that in regarding Music from the point of view occupied by this work, we do not discover it in its technical and mechanical details. We regard it as an astronomer, a heavenly body; not so much to unfold its individual principles, as to discover those great laws that bind it to the universe; to trace the spring of its orbit, and the influence it exerts upon, and receives from, the other influences in the mental concave. Its surface aspect is not again gone over; but its rise from the general human horizon is endeavoured to be traced, and its power, brightness, and ultimate effect as a light in the moral firmament of man, revealed.

Therefore, although the present work on account of its subject (and as tending, by connecting in a near relationship that subject with some of the most momentous, moral, and intellectual phenomena of man, to lift up the art of music, to a lofty and dignified position in general estimation), recommends itself specially to the musician; still it solicits the attention of all who are interested in the philosophy of art generally; and through the light it endeavours to throw upon common human phenomena, the laws of the mind, the evolution of the feelings, and the principles of moral demonstration; in the subjects with which it has presumed to cope, it applies to all who possess emotion and employ a language.

The three essays which constitute the work, should be perused in the order in which they appear, as that is the order in which they were written. Many of the principles laid down in their course, falling into connection with those previously established; as the mind in proceeding from a certain starting point is often led, in threading the vale of thought, into a channel of reflection issuing from a totally different and former starting point of inquiry, and is thus augmented in its progress, and confirmed in the direction it was pursuing.

J. G.

THE RELATIONSHIP OF MUSIC TO THE OTHER FINE ARTS.

EMOTION AROUSED BY INFLUENCES APPEALING TO THE MORAL NATURE WILL EXPRESS ITSELF THROUGH THE MORE ELEVATED DEMONSTRATIVE FACULTIES.—NO DEMONSTRATION OF WHATEVER ORDER CAN BE EFFECTED EXCEPT THROUGH THE INSTRUMENTALITY, MORE OR LESS, OF SOME PHYSICAL FACULTY.—EMOTIONS OF A SPIRITUAL CHARACTER IN BEING DEMONSTRATED, *i.e.* "PHYSICALLY TRANSLATED," MUST IN THIS PROCESS UNDERGO GREATER TRANSFORMATION THAN THOSE OF A LESS ELEVATED NATURE.—THE ACT OF THIS TRANSFORMATION IS ART.—THE PROCESS INSTINCTIVELY ADOPTED BY THE FACULTIES OF MAN IN THE EXPRESSION OF EMOTION CONSISTS OF THE IMITATION OR REPRODUCTION OF ITS EXTERNAL INFLUENCES.—THIS PROCESS IS A MENTAL INSTINCT OF SELF-SUSTAINMENT.—ALL EXPRESSION ATTAINED THROUGH THE ARTS OF POETRY AND PAINTING IS CONSUMMATED THROUGH THE PRINCIPLE OF "IMITATION."—MUSIC DIFFERS FROM THE ABOVE-MENTIONED, AND ALL OTHER, ARTS, IN THE RESPECT THAT ITS EMOTIONAL EXPRESSION IS NOT CONSUMMATED THROUGH THE ABOVE PRINCIPLE, BUT THROUGH SOME DEEPER ONE.—THE HARMONY OF THE CREATURE WITH CREATION, THE GENERAL CAUSE OF THE RAPTURE OF LIFE.—THIS HARMONY REALIZED BY THE MORAL NATURE OF MAN, INDUCES THAT GENERAL FLOW OF INTELLECTUAL ACTIVITY, AND OF EMOTIONAL DEMONSTRATION WHICH EVER ATTENDS HUMANITY, AND WHICH EMBRACES ART, LITERATURE, AND RELIGION.—EMOTIONS, THOUGH MOSTLY AROUSED SUCCESSIVELY, MAY EXIST IN THE NATURE SIMULTANEOUSLY.—MUSIC CAN EXPRESS THIS LATTER CONDITION OF THE BREAST IN ONE GENERAL ARTISTIC EXHIBITION.—EMOTIONS, OF THE INFLUENCES OF WHICH THEIR POSSESSOR IS UNCONSCIOUS, CAN BE IMPARTED THROUGH THE MEDIUM OF MUSIC.—THE DEFINITE MISSION OF ART.

I.

THE RELATIONSHIP OF MUSIC TO THE OTHER FINE ARTS.

WHEN some particular beauty, excellence, or charm is marked by one with faculties adapted for the full perception of that peculiar merit, and the observer is impelled to express in some manner, by sound, sign, gesture, or language, his inward satisfaction and admiration; it will be found that in the proportion that whatever influences the feelings appeals to the sensual nature, and leaves unaffected the moral system; so will the emotional expression be mostly effected by the common physical faculties, or by the rarer, moral, and intellectual ones.

But the indicative impulse attending all emotion, consisting of a tendency both to express and to impart, involves to a certain extent, in either of these processes, the instrumentality of physical faculty. It will, therefore, be perceived that emotions of a lofty and spiritual character, which live amidst the fine perceptive faculties; in assuming expressional form, in becoming imparted through the medium of the external sense; must in this physical translation employ a different and more removed order of faculties, and thus undergo *greater transformation* than emotions of a less elevated nature; the seat of whose existence lies closer to the demonstrative faculties of man.

Now, the act of this transformation, the process of converting an inward emotion into a palpable influence is Art, and the faculty that accomplishes it is Genius.

The term beauty is one that admits of great adaptability in its application. Sometimes it is used only as the name for what is agreeable and lovely in outward appearance. But I propose to use it in its boundless and lofty sense, as the symbol for that divine charm which inspires so warmly within us the instinct of admiration whenever we contemplate what is wise, skilful, or good. It is this principle of beauty visible in some definite shape, that inspires those feelings in the human breast which express themselves in the language of art.

Now, it will be observed, that whenever some external influence arouses in the breast ideas of love, admiration, or devotion; the first spontaneous tendency of these ideas, their first expression, will be to *imitate* and partially reproduce *the influence that created them;* and that throughout all the varied walks of the human mind, in the embodiment, in a sensible form, of an emotional idea, this remarkable principle of "imitation" continually prevails.

It is for example conspicuously illustrated in considering the mental process of the Painter, whose mind being peculiarly adapted for the due appreciation of the principle of beauty, as revealed in nature's external form, arrangement, and effect; no sooner meets it than the emotion it arouses impels him to *imitate* the generating influence, by reproducing upon canvass those particular natural effects, through which this pervading principle first revealed itself to him.

The Poet also, in the expression of emotion derived from the above order of influence, would *reproduce* it by description, as the artist by representation. This character of beauty, however, does not solely constitute the poetical sphere of contemplation. The poet's mind being more fully sensitive to the solemn beauty revealed in the action of the sentiments and passions of the human breast.

Yet in these circumstances, still in obedience to the above tendency to imitation, he is impelled, in the capacity of the dramatist, to create scenes, circumstances, incentives, and characters—to form the inscrutable and complicated apparatus of life, and thus *again excite to visible action* the mystic phenomenon of human passion.

This imitative tendency of the human feelings is nothing more than a mental instinct of self-sustainment. The process that a feeling of a warm and ardent character naturally adopts in order to perpetuate its existence.

Now, the sphere of contemplation occupied by the mind of the Poet and the Musician, is to a great extent the same. The minds of both being specially sensitive to the interest revealed in the action of the human passions and sentiments. But their mode of demonstrating and imparting the emotions thus acquired is dissimilar.

For, whereas the Poet creates a certain emotion in another by reproducing its immediate cause, its external influence. Whereas he exhibits its character and intensity, by depicting its effects, which are all but the outward indicative signs of that emotion. Music does not; but renders by a medium of expression peculiar to herself—namely, melody and rhythm, a nearer attribute of the hidden feeling, than are any of its outward and palpable indications. And though on this account the emotion so expressed may not be so obvious and distinct to the immediate sense, as when interpreted by the other arts, still for the same reason it is realized more deeply and intensely to the moral perception.

From the foregoing remarks then it will be perceived that, whereas all other languages of Art endeavour to reproduce that influence, that phase of beauty that called them to action, by the principle of *imitation*,—by copying and representing the different external marks, signs, and attributes of the above influence. Music does not. Her development of the great principle of beauty is by pure and abstract *expression*. By a mystic, original, and fervid influence " without a name."

Within every creature that a beneficent Creator has called to existence, he has also implanted a feeling of pleasure in that existence, a sustained, healthy, and abiding joy; not traceable to any one of the prominent worldly incitements of this emotion, but the genial result of the exquisite adaptation of the creature to all the surrounding influences in creation. The fervent and deep-seated rapture of life, which at times may appear to be warped by misfortune, whilst, in truth, it is this which softens adversity, and that can only become totally eradicated and benumbed by sin.

In inferior animals this pleasure, in simply

being, is rendered apparent solely by the general character of their outward demeanour—as by the fluttering ecstacy of the bird of the air as it sings or flies, or by the calm placidity and contentment of the beast of the earth—calm, complacent, and comfortable, even to gracefulness. But when this great principle of harmony, arising from the adaptability of nature within to nature without, is not entirely left to the tardy response of the grosser animal faculties. When it is more acutely perceived and more vividly felt by aid of the bright light of human reason. When the eloquent and overwhelming influences in surrounding nature realize their adaptability to man's moral, as well as to his physical being, then a far deeper and more intelligent rapture is created, and by far more fervent, lofty, and spiritual, is the expression thereof. For it is this expression that is the name for all that mental and moral phenomena which throughout the history of the world has ever exalted and rendered glorious the existence of the human race. It is the ardent spiritual glow, aroused by the influences in surrounding nature, striking the expectant and attuned senses of the breast of man; that has charged his whole nature with that ennobling restlessness; that aspiring energy and intellectual desire, which has incited him to the pursuit of knowledge. Which has warmed him to pour forth the appealings of art. Which has moulded his judgment to the love of virtue, and which has assisted his consciousness in the reception of religion.

When we consider how variedly beautiful and different in character are the things that Providence has ordained shall influence mankind; how comprehensive is the extent of human faculties appealed to; how limited the extent allotted to one man—and how this extent thus allotted may be not only of a different character in different natures, but of a greater or a lesser intensity where it is of the same character. We shall not find it difficult to account for the many different phases that the expression of human emotions assumes; nor for the different degrees of intensity and impressiveness possessed by expressions belonging to the same phase.

It has been observed that a work of art is in most cases the imparting to others an inward rapture, by artistically reproducing before them the influences that kindled that rapture; and thus awakening in them a feeling of a like nature.

Now when, through a certain comprehensiveness of appreciation in the beholder, this rapture becomes *compound* in constitution (that is, when it is kindled by influences of a varied character); it will be seen that by those arts of which the expressions, are strictly *definite,* and *externally imitative,* it cannot be wholly uttered in one grand and simultaneous appeal. Because, by such arts, influences of a varied character cannot be reproduced simultaneously and in the same work. Thus, neither by the Painter, nor the descriptive Poet, can the wild beauty of the tempest and the mild beauty of the calm be represented *simultaneously.* Consequently, however abounding may be the nature of the inward glow; by these arts, it cannot be revealed wholly and immediately in all its original fulness and grandeur, but must undergo division and be produced in detail.

We now meet with a second specific attribute of the art of Music. Another remarkable distinction between this and all other, mediums of artistic expression. For Music possesses the peculiar glory of being adapted to express in one *simultaneous* appeal that comprehensive internal grandeur of feeling kindled in a great nature by the mingled eloquence of *all* the exalting influences that beam around him.

The reason of this is, that by the externally imitative arts certain influences are reproduced by representing those influences as they occur *in nature*. Consequently those only can be displayed at the same time whose simultaneous presence is in accordance with natural propriety and physical law. Whilst, on the other hand, the musician, in imparting certain emotions, being free from the necessity of reproducing the influences of these emotions (but relying more for expression in a direct appeal from the emotion itself), is also free to exceed the limits that such a physical necessity, entails.

For although all impressions are given *successively* as the varied influences from the panorama of life affect us, still these impressions may exist within us *simultaneously*, and not only exist simultaneously, but become more deep and intense through this simultaneous existence; because all impressions received from certain points of the universe must become more faithful, clear, and vivid, when placed in immediate contrast with impressions received from other points. Thus the impression produced by a tempest must be more forcible within us when we still retain the impression produced by a calm. Now, it is obvious, that an art that imparts impressions by *representing* in their original and natural form the first influences which excited those impressions, imparts these feelings as they were originally aroused, that is, *successively*. Whilst an art that needs not to follow each impression to its separate influence in external nature, but possesses a language subtle and refined enough to throw the inward impression *direct* to the regarder, and imbue him with it, I say such an art, and Music is one, can impart the above-mentioned combination of impressions—the emotions that have been deepened and vivified by contrast, that have been corrected, elevated, and extended by the judgment,—I say that Music can impart this vague ecstacy in one appropriate and immediate effort.

By these remarks it is not meant to be implied that of all the fine arts Music alone can impart to the regarder's consciousness diversified impressions at the same time. On the other hand, the meditative poet, who, in the action of various natural facts discovers certain considerations through which beauty, in different phases, may be discerned (as it is a property of the human mind to grasp opposing considerations at the same instant,) is enabled by placing these considerations before the attention to reveal the varied beauties they contain, and thus kindle in the regarder impressions of a different character, simultaneously.

Also the poet, the influences of whose rapture

are the beauties revealed in the action of the human passions (as there are no feelings of howsoever opposite a character that may not through connecting circumstances manifest themselves at the same time), is likewise enabled by a judicious arrangement of the circumstances, interests, and incentives of life; affecting actors of a certain character, and occupying a peculiar relationship, to exhibit to the beholder those varied sentiments and passions, in each of which is a beauty of a pleasing, a sacred, a solemn, or an awful character; and thus inspire different impressions simultaneously.

But the object has been to show how Music (that in the expression of an inward ardour is totally *free from the necessity of imitating the outward and natural aspect of the influences that aroused it*, in order to excite a like ardour in others; and that relying more for expression on a vivid appeal in its own original language, *direct* from the feeling itself—an appeal that most mysteriously, yet certainly, bears in it the character and image of the sentiment from which it sprung, and impresses that image upon the consciousness of others)—how Music, through its thus more rarefied medium of expression, its more spiritual language, is peculiarly adapted to express, even in *one effort*, that mingled grandeur of spirit, that wide consciousness of general and eternal worth and beauty, which successive contemplations of the Universe must produce in a nature of enlarged appreciation.

I now proceed to treat of another remarkable consideration connected with this part of the subject.

It is, that the above mentioned ardent condition of the feelings may both exist, and be imparted (by music) *latently;* that is, the process of its formation occurring quite unconsciously to the possessor, who, in this case, is unaware of all concerning it, except of a desire for expression,—of what, as yet, he knows not.

This occurs when the appeal of certain external influences is responded to by the inward consciousness, without their being aroused, a noticeable action of the *mind*, even, as we may admire, reverence, or love, without knowing it.

It is this condition of the feelings which at times impels the impassioned votary of art to sit down to write, paint, or compose, without any definite object; that is, without having any idea prominent or uppermost in his mind that particularly calls for development.

And I believe it is this state of the breast that is intended to be expressed by the term (when used with regard to the fine arts) "inspired."

Now, when this exists in a nature whose medium of expression is the poetic, it will remain thus hidden and pent until some particular one of the surrounding influences is accidentally brought in contact with the mind, thereby causing a more prominent appeal to be exerted on the appreciation by this, than by the other influences, and ending in the expression of the corresponding emotion aroused by this influence prior to the expression of the emotions kindled by the other influences, that are all in like manner successively or simultaneously reproduced as they come in conspicuous contact with the mind.

But owing to the before-mentioned peculiarity of the Musical medium of expression, its being independent of representing in their natural aspect the influences of the emotions it proposes to impart —owing to its remarkable property of throwing, in an original and beautiful language, a faithful impress of those emotions *direct* to the surrounding regarders. Owing to these things, it will be seen that such latent condition of the inward rapture may be imparted by the Musician—possessor *still in its latent and undefined state*, and without the above explained conspicuous interference of the mind.

Still the feelings of the Musician are not always

expressed in this undefined and simultaneous manner, but, through a more prominent action of the mind on one of the external influences, the corresponding emotion kindled by this influence will become more intense and distinct, and thus be quite consciously imparted according to the process of the Musical medium of expression. For as we have a composition expressive of an indefinite grandeur of the breast arising from many, and mingled feelings; as the "Symphony" of abstract expression. So have we also the work of a peculiar meaning, the pourtrayal of a positive and distinct impression—an impression which the composer is mentally conscious of—as the Symphony of Description, the Characteristic Chorus, the Song of Praise, or the Hymn of Supplication.

Now it will be observed, that, through the process of the formation of all non-musical works of art, the *intention* of those works—that is the feeling, or feelings, meant to be imparted—is always distinctly betrayed, whether in the works this original intention be fully attained or not. Because the influences of the emotions to be imparted, being by those arts reproduced in their *natural aspect*, they are immediately recognised, betraying to the regarder whatever emotions such influences when in their proper form, are calculated to inspire.

Thus: when we behold a picture pourtraying an angry and convulsed ocean, a dun and wild canopy, with bleak and massive rocks, we know that the emotion which the artist *intended* to impart was that of a solemn and shocked admiration for the more gloomy and powerful aspects of the Universe. We know this, however little the artist's reproduction of such influences may impress us with this feeling, because we know what feelings those influences, when in their natural state, or when worthily represented, are adapted to excite.

This is also the case in the composition of music, when of a *characteristic* form, although the intention of the piece is not betrayed in its structure, but through other circumstances attending it of a purposely explanatory nature, such as the "words" in vocal, and the characteristic "title" in instrumental, music.

From the foregoing remarks, it will be seen that, in estimating the *merit* of all such productions, a certain guidance is supplied by a comparison drawn between their *intention* and how far this intention is realized in its artistic expression.

But the musical composition of an *uncharacteristic* form, of a wider grasp and more compound character, being the simultaneous outburst of feelings of whose influences the possessor himself is not immediately conscious, and of which the regarder can have no knowledge whatever, can offer no such criterion to the discernment.

And it may be observed, in passing, that this fact accounts for a great abuse of one of the highest forms of musical composition — the symphonic form. For this form of composition, being the expression of certain combined emotions, yet not betraying previously the particular character of those emotions to assist in determining the faithfulness of this expression, offers a comparatively safe opportunity for the empty and pretending to hold up to the worship of mankind works assuming to mean everything, yet meaning nothing.

It is a deep evidence that an enlarged emotional consciousness in the author is the real lofty source of works of art, of the comprehensive order of which we have been speaking. I say it is a deep evidence of this, that the effect of such works most certainly kindles this remarkable *breadth of susceptibility* within their hearers. For in being wrought upon by such works, although no solitary emotion is distinctly impressed, still, in the whole range of moral conception, there exists no feeling that at such a moment the nature is not more susceptible of receiving than at any other time. At such a moment we feel ourselves unaccountably imbued with feelings of Faithfulness, of Sympathy, of Pity, of Ardour, of Heroism, which pass stealthily, but perceptibly, through the wrapt and responsive breast.

Now when, during this phenomenon, an unconscious action of the imagination takes place, the feelings thus imparted will then seem to become attended with such physical circumstances as the condition of our own moral interests would naturally supply. Thus, if within the listener's breast an emotion like Sympathy were inspired, then, through an unconscious action of his imagination, an illustration of this feeling would arise, perhaps in the form of a mother, sister, or friend. This emotion and image would then be succeeded by another, and another,—

> "Till glimpses more sublime
> Of things unseen before,
> Unto the wondering eyes reveal."

And thus would all that is illustrative of the great principle of Beauty in the moral or physical world now reveal itself momentarily and mysteriously to the startled mind.

The above emotions, springing up either with or without attendant circumstances, must not be confounded with those *past feelings* and occurrences that are faintly recalled by the accidental remembrance of something associated with them. For this latter phenomenon is the *recollection* of *old* feelings and circumstances that once actually existed, and personally interested us, and that might have been recalled by any influence whatsoever; whilst the former is a *new* train of emotions kindled within us by the force of an influence which bears the impress of, and which springs direct from, these feelings themselves in the breast of the composer.

In the above illustration, the person in whom the feeling of Sympathy is inspired, may hitherto have been a total stranger to such an emotion. He may have possessed the above mentioned objects adapted for its exercise, but may never heretofore have regarded them in the right spirit. Whilst, if the emotions and circumstances inspired by Music were only those aroused by the principle of association, such an example as this could not occur.

We now arrive at a third specific attribute, distinguishing the art of Music from all others. For it will be observed that, whereas the exponents of the other Arts impart a certain feeling by arbitrarily selecting, and placing before the regarder some physical influence adapted to inspire this feeling—thus conveying the natural circumstances attending the emotion first, and *subsequently* the emotion itself—the Musician imparts the feeling *in the first place;* leaving it to the regarder's moral choice to subsequently enrobe it in whatsoever physical circumstance may interest him the most.

In the inner and moral relationship of Music to the other Fine Arts, we perceive, then, three prominent distinctions. In the first place, we see that, whereas all other artistic impresses, in assuming expressional form, endeavour to reproduce that phase of beauty which created them, by copying its different external signs and attributes, that of Music assumes an *independent form of influence;* and relies for multiplying itself on others—for, perpetuating its existence—not upon the principle of *imitation,* but upon a deeper principle of *abstract expression.**

In the second place, we observe that, whereas the other Arts (they being externally indicative) must, in the conveyance of an emotion of a *com-*

* This principle is further elucidated in the Essay termed „The Moral Theory of Music."

pound nature—in the imparting of a comprehensive internal grandeur of feeling—to a great extent communicate this internal temper in a *fragmentary manner*. The Art of Music can throw off this vague ecstacy in *one* immediate and appropriate effort.

In the third place, we perceive that, whereas the other Arts, in communicating emotional phenomena, convey the circumstances first and the *emotion afterwards*, Music imparts the emotion in the first place, and *subsequently the circumstances*.

In the course of this inquiry, the terms " Feelings," "Emotions," having frequently been used, it may not be irrelevant to briefly pursue an inquiry into the distinction that exists between the sense in which these terms are used with regard to Art and that in which they are used respecting real life. For all those emotions which kindle, or which are kindled by, works of art, are so different in their nature from the instinctive feelings of real life, that they should not, to express them rightly, be called by the same name. They partake more of the calm and abstract character of thoughts, than of the passionate and momentous nature of feelings; as these latter are produced by those influences in life that personally interest and affect us, and that come close to our heart. Whilst the emotions relative to Art are produced by those influences with which we have no personal sympathy, and which only touch us through the medium of contemplation.

The distinction is the same as that between the feelings of a man *under* the influence of personal bereavement, and those of a stranger who *regards* him.

He, whom the influences of life affect personally, is too much absorbed in *bearing* his feelings, to calmly contemplate the moral interest revealed in their action,—to note the forms of beauty wrought from a furnace that is burning in his own breast.

Neither are such feelings intended to be kindled by works of Art; for although sometimes we hear of the Dramatist, the Poet, the Musician, who draws *tears* from his regarders, yet this is certainly not the right result, nor is this the true intention of the appeal of Art.

The intention of the appeal of Art is to impart to others those feelings derived from the exercise of that high faculty, contemplation. To imbue with these feelings those who, through neglecting to exercise this faculty, would perhaps not otherwise have possessed them; and to render more intense such emotions in those who have.

And as these feelings cannot in many cases, as

we have seen, be imparted without representing before the regarder the particular influences which are under the artist's meditative scrutiny in their natural form (as the human passions, whose action is revealed in the materials of the drama); when the regarder, instead of retaining his position as regarder, and *noting* the pervading beauty revealed in the development of the present influences; allows his imagination to carry him away and *involve* him in the personal interest of what is before him,—until he loves, pities, and weeps. Then, instead of partaking of the elevating and salutary food of thought, he is indulging in an inward luxury, as hurtful to the moral nature as are artificial stimulants to the physical. And as any faculty in the system, when wrought upon by artificial, instead of natural influences, becomes perverse, morbid, and imperfect in its action; so likewise do those sacred nerves of the emotional frame, when profaned by false appeals, become senseless to real calls. So are those eyes, full and flowing over to imaginary sorrows, sterile and tearless to real distress.

Let the intention and mission of Art not be mistaken. For though its influence is to diffuse a softness, to kindle a susceptibility, throughout the whole nature of man. Yet this is more to encourage the growth of thought; to generate due reflection; to open *latent* sympathies; to draw forth new faculties of Taste and Appreciation; than to form itself into a focus of sensational incitement, and beguile to action a flow of personal emotion.

The highest, the brightest, the softest, the true scene of Art is at that moral horizon in Nature where ideal light is shed upon earthly objects below, showing them in their spiritual aspect, and revealing their hidden beauty. And its mission is to let into the mind and heart of man this ideal light, radiating from the spirit of Beauty; through whose medium all things are seen more in their true nature, and by whose aid many objects in life reveal a charm and elicit an interest that otherwise would but swell the dull inertiæ surrounding a contracted moral existence.

THE MORAL THEORY OF MUSIC.

HUMAN SPEECH POSSESSES TWO DISTINCT PROPERTIES, THAT WHICH IMPARTS FACTS AND THAT WHICH IMPARTS FEELINGS.—THOUGH THE CONVEYANCE OF THE LATTER MAY RESULT FROM THE IMPARTING OF THE FORMER, IT NEED NOT NECESSARILY DO SO.—IN SPEECH THEREFORE THERE EXISTS A SPECIAL AGENCY FOR THE PASSAGE OF EMOTION, AND THIS WORKS IN EFFECTS OF TONE, EMPHASIS, AND PAUSE.—"TONE" IN SPEECH IS AN EARLY EXEMPLIFICATION OF THE "MELODY" OF MUSIC.—"SENTENTIAL DESIGN" AND "POETIC RHYTHM" IN LANGUAGE IS THE SAME PRINCIPLE AS THAT WHICH EVOLVES THE "PHRASE" AND "TIME" OF MUSIC.—THE MATERIAL CIRCUMSTANCES SURROUNDING THIS PRINCIPLE IN ITS PROGRESS FROM SPEECH TO SONG CONSIDERED.—THE MORAL CIRCUMSTANCES CONSIDERED.—MUSICAL EXPRESSION EXPLAINED.—ITS SPECIAL FUNCTION DEFINED.—THE EXTRAORDINARY IMPRESSIVENESS AND STUPENDOUS EFFECT OF MUSIC IN CERTAIN OF ITS FORMS, AS IN THAT OF SACRED MUSIC, ENDEAVOURED TO BE ACCOUNTED FOR (AN IMPRESSIVENESS AND AN EFFECT SO GREAT AND HIGH AS TO BE AN ANOMALY IN ART).—MORAL CONSIDERATIONS SUGGESTED.

II.

THE MORAL THEORY OF MUSIC.

WHEN one of the many and various influences that continually surround humanity occupies such a close relationship with the nature of man as to personally affect it, such an influence will always produce within this nature a certain fresh impression, some internal flow of feeling more or less abiding, agreeable, or elevated.

Now, as throughout the great realm of humanity, such an action as this is continually going on, and as amidst all mankind there exists a strong and unremitting tendency to express the inward feelings, and a mutual necessity to convey the various facts and occurrences, and thus to diffuse the different influences of emotion, in life; as in short it is a remarkable property of humanity to both physically and morally associate,—it will be observed that every communication from human lips, to effect its due result upon the hearer, must contain two distinct constituent elements— namely, the mechanical symbols or words of exactly defined power, and the free tone, emphasis, and pause, of power indefinite and unprescribed;

the serviceable office fulfilled by the former being to convey the abstract facts that were to be imparted, and that of the latter to express the feelings and impressions those facts previously aroused in the narrator.

Thus, suppose a person to be relating to another the occurrence of some catastrophe in which the narrator was himself involved, and that this catastrophe were a shipwreck. His *words* would impart the abstract facts that happened, but the gradations of *Tone* in which he uttered them, the striking *Emphasis*, and the effective *Pause*, would convey the Feelings he experienced through the scene he is recording, in the temperament of which he is now relating it; so that the listener, as well as becoming acquainted with the abstract facts that occurred, would at the same time be also impressed with the emotions of awe and anguish that the actual presence of these facts aroused in the breast of the narrator, and thus become possessed of a more faithful and vivid idea of the distant catastrophe itself, and of a deeper sympathy for the interests therein involved. From this then it appears that although the bare knowledge of the abstract circumstances and truths of some important occurrence will (through the susceptibility of the great nerve of sympathy running throughout all humanity) inspire appropriate feelings in those who did not witness or were not immediately affected by the above occurrence, that still, in order that the intercommunication of the many momentous events in life *shall* duly impress even those whose individual interests were not perceptibly affected by such influences, and that there may be some provision to gratify man's continual desire to express his feelings ; that in response to these considerations, human speech has been inspired with another property besides that of imparting abstract facts, namely the property of imparting the feelings and impressions that these facts previously aroused in the breast of the narrator.

This important *second property* of human speech is, as I said before, verbally defined by the terms Tone, Emphasis, and Pause, and as a remarkable evidence how faithfully and mysteriously these attributes of speech *do* convey the state of feeling in which it is uttered, it will be remembered that a listener may oftentimes through their influence alone become possessed of appropriate feelings and partially surmise the attending facts even when these facts themselves have not been formally betrayed.

Yet this emotional property attending human speech is not only serviceable to man in expressing such emotions as generally and obviously accompany the knowledge and experience of certain facts, but it is of further assistance to him in imparting those inward feelings accompanying certain facts, —which feelings, though they are calculated to be aroused by the experience of the above facts still do not always attend it.

For when we consider that of all in the vast multitude of truths that are, there exists but very few the complete importance of which, the exact extent of whose influence, in short, whose real nature is wholly known; we shall perceive that through the extent of the influence of these truths being undefined, so likewise must the possible *results* of their unknown influence—so likewise must their possible impressions upon Humanity—be also variable and indefinite; and that therefore the same fact existing in different minds may in each several case exist in a different phase and thus be *not exactly the same fact*. Now, as the ordinary symbols of speech are only calculated to represent the same fact according to two or three different perceptions of it, it follows, that in order to impart even *facts themselves as existing in different minds*, a further and finer medium of expression, a medium more adaptive in representing the delicate distinctions in our perception of facts, is required than the common and general materials of human speech.

In these circumstances then, in communications of this character, we meet with the property under consideration occupying a position of increased importance in the constitution of human speech. For it is these finer distinctions in our perception of truths, it is such distinction as perhaps exists but in one mind's perception of a truth, it is how certain truths impress the individual alone, in distinction to how they may impress others, that the property in speech of Tone Emphasis and Pause, is peculiarily adapted to impart. Although I have spoken of this property under consideration as being an extension of human speech, it will at the same time be perceived that it is still a distinct Principle from that of ordinary human language; because all impressions imparted by the latter are conveyed by the principle of Association, that is, by the directing in the mind of the listener an appeal to his experience; or else by the principle of Representation, that is, the reproducing (either by description or exhibition) those influences themselves that in the first case affected the speaker. In both of these processes it will be observed there is a *repetition in the case of the listener of the same operation that previously occurred within the speaker* when he himself became emotionally impressed.

Now it is evident that the impressions imparted

by Tone, Emphasis, and Pause, when acting in their peculiar capacity, explained as in the last paragraph but one, are not conveyed by the principle of Association; because such impressions as these exist in the mind of the speaker *alone*, and could not be found in the experience of the listener. It is also obvious that impressions imparted by this property are not conveyed by the principle of representation; because the effects of "tone," "emphasis," and "pause," appeal too exclusively to the finer appreciative faculties to be reducible to stereotpyed symbols of representation, available for the reproduction of palpable influences; but, on the other hand, they are the improvised but instinctively recognised reflections of *impressions themselves*, thus conveyed *direct* from their possessor.

This remarkable property under consideration is, then, an original and mysterious influence, whose especial attribute it is to impart those particular ideas and impressions that are peculiar to only one mind's perception of any circumstance, truth, or occurrence. It is an eloquent and ethereal attribute with which the Creator has inspired the language of Man, to kindle and awaken his sympathies to the due response of that which appeals to them (thus materially furthering that inward process by which he becomes possessed of common emotions)—to be the only imbuer of particular emotion, and the sole medium of *direct expression* and relief for all emotion.

Now I shall endeavour to show in the following pages, that this property in human speech of Tone, Emphasis, and Pause, is the first indication we perceive in Nature of that principle which in a higher stage of development constitutes the effect termed " Music." I shall endeavour to trace this remarkable principle from its first faint indications in human speech, through the various circumstances attending its onward progress, past the gradually more conspicuous and elaborate exemplifications it assumes in its upward course, to its kingly and overpowering effects in Music.

By so doing I shall be able, through pointing out that intelligible function and definite meaning, which is easily perceived in the early and simple exemplifications of this principle, to account also for many of those remarkable effects of its after fulness and maturity in Music, that have been hitherto deemed inexplicable, which have hitherto been classed with the isolated truths of our nature that betray no connection with those primary and general principles that are the materials of human reason, and which, therefore, have hitherto been supposed to admit of no analysis.

I shall endeavour to show that that principle from which the attribute of human speech, "tone," emanates, is—Melody. And that the principle from which the "emphasis" and "pause," of human language proceeds is—Phrase; which two principles understood in a duly wide sense constitute the complete effect "Music." That wide sense above alluded to, in which I have employed the terms Melody and Phrase, is, Melody, *inclusive* of those progressions and effects of Harmony, which the existence of Melody naturally involves; and Phrase inclusive of those systematic effects of Rhythm which are exemplifications of the same property. These considerations lead me before I proceed with the main line of argument representing the principal intention of this Essay, to make a few brief remarks concerning the above conjoined properties —namely, Melody, Harmony, Phrase, and Time, representing in reality but two principles, into which the effect "Music" has been artificially divided.

Many principles of which man becomes cognisant, and effects of which he becomes conscious, however consistent, positive and perfect their influence appears, are nevertheless, by the exercise of due observation, discovered to be the result of the action of a certain number of minor principles, and the consequence of a peculiar intermixture of minor effects.

And these minor principles and effects, though they are in truth but component parts of one great principle or effect, though the precise limits of their interdiffusion, as in the colours of the rainbow, cannot be determined, may nevertheless be seen to betray a partial individuality.

But for convenience in investigating the nature of general principles or effects, these minor parts they contain have been artificially separated, and considered as *distinct* divisions.

Now reflecting that it is quite impossible to perceive how much the function of one of the minor parts of the great principle (when in combined action with the rest) is constituted by the hidden action of the others; or how much one minor effect (as exemplified in the grand effect) latently includes that of the others;—it is obvious that the *exact relationship* of the minor parts of any great principle or effect, when in combined action, is totally imperceptible. Therefore, in the consideration of any grand principle or effect, when we meet with the above definite lines of separation and distinct divisions, we should always remember that such *definite* lines are *artificial*, and that such *distinct* divisions are only *so considered*. Consistent with the above remarks, the principle of "Music" has been seen to consist of four conjoined, but at the same time partially individual, minor principles, and has therefore been *considered* to be the result of the *distinct* divisions — Melody, Harmony, Phrase, and Rhythm. But in the investigations of musical works—in the forming of ideas on the constitution of Music, it has not been sufficiently remembered that Music is only *considered* to be constituted by these four *distinct* divisions:— that these divisions, though betraying partial individuality, are nevertheless interdiffused so remarkably and mysteriously as to attain to unity, and that there can be no effect whatever contained in "Music" that does not in some proportion include them all. I mean by these remarks, that in the analysis of musical compositions and effects, a consciousness of this undefined separation—of this separated mersion—of the minor principles (attained by close observation) has not been sufficiently betrayed. Nor has their partial individuality (apparent by a broader glance) been fairly or proportionately represented.

All musicians who have explored the moral nature of their art must be aware how, through these,

THE MORAL THEORY OF MUSIC.   51

thus imperfect, representations made by the generality of the exponents of the musical art, the most erroneous ideas of its true nature have been created, and still prevail. How little the remarkable and beautiful closeness of relationship of the principles of harmony and melody—melody and time—harmony and phrase (exemplified when such combinations of principles appear severally the most conspicuous ones in the musical effect) is duly realised.

But not only has the *affinity* of these principles been imperfectly represented, but their *contrast* likewise has not by far been adequately betrayed. Not only, examining them minutely, is the closeness of their relationship imperfectly understood: but, regarding them more comprehensively, those distinctions betrayed by their partial individuality—the proportions of their contrast—is also not duly appreciated.

Thus, whilst the general perceptions of persons concerning each one of the principles, Melody, Harmony, Phrase, and Rhythm, *with regard to the others*, have been allowed to become divided into four distinct ideas, ideas inevitably narrowed and impoverished through this unnatural separation; so, likewise, amidst the majority of minds, has the appreciation of the relative proportion and importance of each of these four principles, *with regard to the one grand effect of Music*, become greatly warped and contracted.

Concerning this latter point, it suffices at present to remark, how inadequately the due proportion and importance of the principles Time and Phrase, to the complete effect " Music," has been hitherto represented. How inordinately prominent, in the production of Musical effect, have been hitherto deemed the principles of Melody and Harmony, to the exclusion, as but subordinate agents, of the principles "Time" and " Phrase." How the principle " Time" has been considered to fulfil only a mechanical function, and how the principle of Phrase has been almost totally forgotten.*

* The effect of many of Handel's chorusses, the greatest effects that music has risen to, is almost wholly produced through the principle of "Phrase,"—the æsthetic grouping of simple masses of harmony, the rhythmical design wrought with abstract fragments of Tone. Take for example the chorus "He gave them hailstones." Where is the effect of melody? Is the blending of the sounds,—the harmony, a noticeable feature in the effect? Do effects of modulation enhance in any considerable degree the grandeur? The source of this grandeur is consequently nearly solely constituted by the principle of "Phrase." It will be observed also that it is this principle in music more than melody which lends itself to the expression of the sublime, and I think it is the faculty of wielding this principle more than the faculty of melody,

Now the particular connection of these two latter principles with regard to each other, and also their individual function and importance with regard to the grand effect of Music, will be rendered clearly apparent in the course of those arguments that will constitute the principal portion of this essay. For the present, let it suffice for me to remark, that it is chiefly through the consideration of this principle of "phrase" that we are enabled to discover the presence of the Musical principle, in other and extraneous effects, from its partial indications, diversified throughout Converse Oratory and Poetry, to its complete and unalloyed presence in Music.

Concerning the true relationship of the principles melody and harmony, it will not be necessary for me to expatiate very lengthily, because correct ideas on this subject are at length becoming formed and duly disseminated.

That the hitherto generally adopted definitions of melody and harmony are shallow and imperfect, is evident from even a cursory consideration of them. For to define Melody as a *succession* of single sounds, and Harmony as a *combination* of sounds, is only to define those principles in their mechanical shape

harmony, or any other principle of music that is the test of the highest order of musical genius; witness Handel and Beethoven.

and outward appearance, whilst an intelligible definition of the *effect* termed Melody in distinction to the *effect* termed Harmony is still unpresented.

Now when we consider that an æsthetical and a definite impression cannot possibly be solely produced by a succession of single notes—that whenever we become conscious of such an impression, seemingly so derived, the succession of sounds is only its immediate fountain; its real source being those progressions of harmony of which this succession of sounds *is the most conspicuous part*, and which it rapidly, unconsciously, but positively suggests; the truth of this being exemplified in the fact that those breasts to whom melody imparts the most meaning—in whom it produces the most intelligible and exalted impression—are always found to be most susceptible to the conception of harmony;—when we consider these circumstances, we clearly perceive that the effect *termed* Melody is, in truth, the effect *of* Harmony.

Again, when we consider that neither can an æsthetical nor a definite impression be solely created by a stationary combination of sounds, that whenever we become conscious of such an impression, seemingly so derived, the real source from which it flows, is that *understood progression of harmony* in which this isolated group of sounds is but a passing wave, for progression is in the very nature of Harmony, as "motion" is of Life;—when we consider these circumstances we also perceive that the " effect" termed Harmony is in truth the effect of a *progression* of combined sounds. But from the preceding considerations it appears that the effect termed Melody is the same, only with the peculiarity that such effect is suggested by the particular force of one part of the combined progression, instead of being equally expressed by each.

From these considerations, then, we learn that when we regard the principles melody and harmony in their "effect" (which is their life), and not in their mechanical "shape" (which is their body), we find them to be the same thing;—we see the universality of their inter-diffusion, and at the same time the true distinction, such as it exists, between them. We find that the unity they constitute is a progression of combined sounds, and that as this unity assumes the effect of Harmony, or the effect of Melody, occurs respectively as it comes in contact with the appreciation, equally, or with one part more prominent:—when it meets the mind as an elevation, or *in perspective*.

The "effects," which have been spoken of as of Melody, or of Harmony, must be still understood to be the result of *all* the four musical principles, Melody, Harmony, Phrase, and Rhythm. They are only spoken of as effects of melody or of harmony, as these principles become respectively the most conspicuous ones of the whole combination. It being impossible, in regarding the nature of the several minor principles of music, to exemplify such particular ones as may be under consideration, more distinctively than in that combination with the four, wherein they appear most conspicuous.

Thus there is no such effect in music as a distinct effect of melody, harmony, phrase, or rhythm. These four minor principles betray a partial individuality, and assume ever varying proportions in the one grand principle of Music. Still music has no "*branches;*" it has numberless different *aspects* in each of which its constituent principles are ever omnipresent; and whenever we meet with a musical effect termed Melody or Harmony, we must always remember that it is the above mentioned, single grand effect, that is, in reality, intended to be expressed, only with the peculiarity of such minor principle as is mentioned constituting the *greater portion* of its aspect.

When music assumes the form of "song," we regard it in its aspect of Melody; yet harmony, phrase, and rhythm are still moving and glowing in the back ground. When it steals devotionally upon us in its effect of the "organ voluntary," we mark it in its aspect of Harmony; nevertheless melody, phrase, and rhythm, though receding from the mind in its solemn conception, still at times betray themselves, faintly and fitfully, like the ever quenchless stirrings of the great human heart, breaking into its wrapt contemplation of futurity. When music starts upon us in its inspiriting effect of the "march," our senses echo to its exemplification of Rhythm. And when it exalts us, rolling by, wrapt in the grandeur of the dramatic or descriptive "chorus," our imagination swells with the sublime impressions of Phrase.

Even regarding these four minor principles—melody, harmony, phrase, and rhythm—as but different aspects of the single effect, Music, it must be remembered, as I have hinted before, that they involve but two really dissimilar points of view, from which we perceive but two principles or aspects—namely, *tone* and *phrase*. The division of the first of these betraying melody and harmony, and that of the last, rhythm and phrase.

I now proceed in my previously announced intention of tracing these minor principles, melody, harmony, phrase, and rhythm, from their extraneous and partial indications in human speech, to the point where they culminate in music.

In regarding the distinction between the sounds of the emotional part of human speech and those of music—in exploring the connexion between language and song—we find that when the intervals, between the sounds of human speech are more *exactly defined*, and the sounds themselves thus rendered more *positive*, that these sounds will become *musical sounds*, suggesting and betraying that remarkable and infinite system of Music to which they belong.

When we observe the aspect of physical nature with the view of discovering those general principles pervading it that render it agreeable and beautiful to man — that form the element of affinity between him and it,—we perceive this moral element to be partly produced through the effects of Nature's infinite arrangements of *colour*, and partly through those of her endless varieties of proportion and physical coincidence. Thus, in admiring a flower, the emotion of admiration is partly produced by the effect of the tints and shades in its colour, and partly by the arrangement of its proportions, the unity, though originality of its design, and the almost exact coincidence of one leaf, petal, or part, with the others.

It will also be observed that in all objects of this nature, these two principles mutually enhance each other—that although they are different in character, they never exist apart, and solitary—that, in fact, where one is, its effect must be enhanced by the presence of the other. Now, the relationship of these two principles in their effect upon the mind through the medium of the eye, is similar to the relationship of Tone (by which term is meant to be expressed the principles of "melody" and "harmony") and Phrase, in their effect upon the mind through the medium of the ear. Phrase, in its action on the ear, conveying the grand outlines of the musical idea, as Form, in its action on the eye, conveys the grand outlines of the artistic idea. And Tone, imparting a soul and perfection to the bold blank space that constitutes phrase, even as Colour imparts the same to the unrelieved surface enclosed by the outlines of form.

I now proceed to trace the evidences of

Phrase from its faint indications in human speech to its forcible and overpowering effects in music.

In human speech, especially in its higher efforts, we first perceive indications of "phrase" in that tendency that the orator betrays to *balance* the different portions of a sentence. Thus in the delivery of some important sentiment or impressive truth, we first detect a distant evidence of the Phrase of music, in that tendency that we see prevailed in the constructor, to cause the spaces that occur between such pauses as the sentence may contain, and also to render those points in the sentence where occurs the effect of emphasis —to bear a peculiar relationship to each other; so that the ear, in receiving the whole impression of the sentence, may become conscious of an effect of emphasis or pause in one part, being peculiarly related, and dependent for due meaning, to a sympathetic effect of emphasis and pause occurring in another part of the sentence.

This principle of Phrase is the conveying a meaning to the mind by means of the more or less forcible impressions produced on the ear by any species of sound, being reduced to a certain arrangement.

For example, the ear of a listener in receiving

the successive impressions imparted by the speaker, must become conscious of some of these impressions being more forcible and intense than others.

Now the principle of Phrase is the arranging of these more prominent impressions, with regard to each other, and to all the minor ones the sentence conveys, in such a manner, as to produce some particular effect within the mind of the listener.

"As Cæsar *loved* me,—I *weep* for him."
* * * * *
* * "his *glory* not extenuated, wherein he was worthy,—nor his *offences* enforced, for which he suffered death."

It may be here opined, that it is the relationship in meaning of the words thus placed in juxtaposition which involves a similar arrangement of Emphasis and Pause. This is true with regard to the speaker. But, with regard to the listener, it will be perceived that it is mainly through the effect of Emphasis and Pause that this particular relationship is communicated, and the meaning thus fully imparted. And, again, few will dispute that there is an *abstract effect* in this use of Emphasis and Pause, clothing the sentence in a vague grandeur, which even of *itself* emits an impressiveness to the hearer, and constitutes a relief to the speaker.

Proceeding further to that form of language in the construction of which the principle of Phrase is more fully developed, and which is allowed to possess the property of expressing human sentiments with remarkable force and fervency—namely, Poetry—we find this principle existing in a more compound and elaborate form, and arrive at the perception of the first important peculiarity in its nature.

For we now become conscious of the impressions produced upon the ear by the effect of emphasis and pause succeeding each other more rapidly, regularly, but more *softly*, — *resulting in the creation of a clear and continued " rhythm,"*—whilst the ear becomes at the same time sensible of the broader outlines of Phrase. Even as, whilst we trace the systematic and minute divisions with which the edges of a leaf are bordered, the eye is at the same time conscious of the two or three larger sections it likewise contains.

Now the effect of Rhythm in poetry is identical with the effect of Time in music; but the peculiar relationship of Rhythm and Phrase in poetry, compared to the relationship of these principles as exemplified in music, involves many distinctions, which will now be considered, and to which the reader's special attention is requested.

THE MORAL THEORY OF MUSIC. 63

In the first place, it will be observed that, in poetry, to each individual accent and fall in the Rhythm, is exactly fitted a syllable of speech: so that the abstract effect produced upon the ear by a succession of syllables, is identical with the effect produced by a succession of accents and falls. Whereas, in music, the abstract effect upon the ear of the successive accents and falls in the Time may be either expressed or *understood*, whilst, at the same time, *other effects may be produced*, whose impressions upon the ear are *not identical* with the successive impressions of the Time, although they are governed by them. For it will be observed that whereas in poetry the smallest and largest effect of accent and fall, is the regular accent and fall of the established time; in music the impressions produced upon the ear by each accent and fall of the time may be either *connected and sustained* into various larger and more deliberate impressions; or *subdivided* into many smaller and more rapid ones.

In the second place it will be observed, that whereas in the construction of poetry whatever may be the length or shape of one phrase, it must be *immediately succeeded by another*. A succeeding phrase must be commenced upon the very next accent or fall to that on which the previous one terminated, or else the idea of the established rhythm will be interrupted or overthrown. Whilst in music the established Time may be permitted to silently yet markedly proceed at the end of one phrase before another is begun, thus bringing in the eloquence of *silence* to throw additional meaning upon the past phrase, and to impart the same to the succeeding one (thus allowing the impression produced by the last phrase to *expand* in this silence of the mind, whilst through the idea of the Time being unremittedly impressed, the appropriate *enthusiasm* of the breast is still sustained); or a succeeding phrase may be commenced upon the next *subdivision* of the regular accent and fall.

Thus the superior development attained by this principle of "phrase" in Music, compared to that attained by it in Poetry, consists in its infinitely greater variety of "Form" (owing to the freedom it there possesses to both commence and terminate upon any minute *subdivision* of the established accent and fall, instead of in its beginning or ending, having to include *one whole accent and fall*).

The variety of "Character," that it may assume; when its Form is decided (owing to its power of rendering the abstract impression upon the ear produced by the whole phrase *otherwise than iden-*

tical with the abstract impression of the collective regular accents and falls, these latter being understood or subordinately expressed from one end of the phrase to the other, whilst at the same time, from the enclosed space, other impressions may be produced, either more sustained or more minute than those of the established accent and fall).

And in its greater Force, Clearness, and Relief of impression, whilst at the same time it is perfectly obedient to the government of the established Rhythm, the impressions of which upon the ear are never for a moment interrupted when the boundaries of the Phrase are defined in the strongest manner; whereas in Poetry the impressions upon the ear, wrought by the established Time, are always interrupted and displaced wherever the boundaries of a Phrase are more than just perceptibly impressed. This distinction between the Phrase of Music and that of Poetry being owing to the fact that the Musical phrase is unrestricted by the necessity that characterises the Poetical one, of immediately succeeding and preceeding other phrases: but on the other hand, as has been before remarked, it is free to commence or end at any distance from them, the eloquence of the intermediate spaces being sustained by *silence*, by the expanded impression in the mind, of the past phrase, the meaning of which is more apparent as its effect is more comprehensive, through being contemplated at this distance, and by the unwaning enthusiasm of the breast; still kept kindled by the unremitted impressions of the Time. But, if on the other hand, the effect upon the listener is to be wrought by phrases immediately succeeding one another, then the liberty that the Musical phrase possesses to commence upon any *subdivision* of the regular accent and fall, enables the phrases of Music to succeed each other even more immediately, as it also enables them to follow one another more deliberately and in a more isolated manner, than can those of poetry.

In pursuing the distinctions here advanced between the "phrase" of Poetry and that of Music, it must be particularly borne in mind that in both cases, the impressions produced upon the ear by the principle of phrase are considered only as *asbstract impressions*. Thus the impressions mentioned as being wrought by the phrase of Poetry, are in the above remarks, supposed to be followed no further than to their first shock of sound upon the ear, and not to their subsequent development into words, and thence to meanings within the mind. And in like manner the impressions mentioned as being produced by the phrase of Music, are in the above considerations, supposed to be followed no further than to their first shock upon the ear, of vague, dead sound, and not to their simultaneous resolution into the intelligible notes of music.

For it is only by considering the effect of Phrase in poetry and music as abstracted from the words in one case, and from the musical sounds in the other, that we are enabled to perceive clearly the unbroken continuation of this principle throughout both arts, and also the exact point, where, in the onward progress of the principle of phrase, the art of Poetry ends and that of Music commences.

In tracing, then, the progress of this principle, we find when it has assumed a compound condition, as in poetry—that is, when we find one series of impressions upon the ear, reduced into the continued and regular effect of " rhythm," and at the same time another broader series of impressions, governed by the previous series, adjusted into the less regular but wider, and still consistent effect of " phrase"—that having attained this condition directly the impressions of the established accent and fall of the Rhythm becomes *subdivided* into smaller and rapider impressions, or *sustained* into longer and more majestic ones; or again, directly the wider series of impressions become *isolated* in their relationship with each other, whilst at the same time the smaller series of impressions continue unremittedly throughout,—that directly this principle of Phrase becomes developed into one of these phases, it demands—through the primary hidden principles of its existence — through the laws of nature—and for the due sustainment of that effect of consistency and intelligibility which Nature enjoins all things to assume, in whatever phase of their existence; for these reasons it here demands the conjunctive presence of *musical* sound.

Before reaching the above-mentioned stages of development, the primary laws that regulate the *aspect* of this principle of Phrase, in its relationship with the appreciation of man, permit its impressions upon the ear to be wrought by that species of sound appropriate for the formation of words, and therefore to the borders of these stages of its development we find that human language in its march of progress conjunctively attends the principle of phrase in the form of Poetry. But directly the principle in question attains the development of the above-mentioned stages of its progress, these same laws that regulate the aspect of all things in connection with the perceptive faculties of man, now enjoin its impressions upon the ear to be wrought by that species of sound appropriate for the production of music; and, therefore, beyond the borders of these stages, we find that human language can never attend it, except the sound which forms it be musical sound.

Thus, if any succeeding, but at the same time, *isolated* phrases be correctly rendered in that species of sound adapted for the formation of the words of speech, the result will be the production of an effect imparting a certain satisfaction through its exemplification of the principle of Phrase; but at the same time through this exemplification being rendered in the species of sound adapted to form ordinary language, and not in that adapted for the formation of music, impressing the most unmistakable conviction of incongruity, and of the violation of the great law of Natural Propriety, which infringement we are always even instinctively conscious of wherever it occurs.

In considering the effect of this example, we find, that although the abstract principle of Phrase is correctly exemplified, still, that it gains no intelligibility—no enhancement of effect—from the conjunctive presence of the sound in which it is rendered; and, also, that the words likewise obtain no further force or efficiency of expression from the conjunctive presence of the principle of Phrase which they embody, but, on the other hand, lose both in intelligibility and efficiency of expression.

It may be here observed that whenever these regular unremitted and smaller series of impressions occur, attended by another series of impressions, broader and more free—whether all these impressions be produced by that species of sound adapted to form words, or by that adapted to form music—whether the result be poetry or music—the assisting function fulfilled in either case by the smaller series of impressions is remarkable and peculiar.

For as the general effect of reiterated, alternated, or of any arrangement of regulated abstract impressions, upon the ear, is to gradually kindle a certain vague mental susceptibility—to awaken the imagination—to excite expectation: so the influence of that systematic and unremitted series of impressions in question upon the hearer, is to *support* that high effort of imagination—to *sustain* that exalted fire of moral excitement invoked within the breast by the passage of the wider and grander series of impressions. The function of this regular and unremitted effect of rhythm is not to produce within the nature any positive and distinct idea, but it is to generate and sustain that vague, undefined, but pervading impression of grandeur in the breast that is indispensable for the due reception, in all their warmth and glory, of truly great and lofty ideas.

From these and the foregoing considerations, we are enabled to observe rather closely the *material* relationship of the art of music to that of poetry, and to perceive exactly the point of conjunction between them. We see at the point in the progress of the principle of Phrase, where it attains that more perfect and elaborate development which demands the conjunctive presence of the musical species of sound—at this point we observe that the art of Poetry ends, and that of Music commences. Regarding both arts as but one grand and continued medium of emotional expression, we see that up to this point it is called "Poetry," and beyond it, "Music."

In surveying the nature of the principle of Tone and Phrase, as betrayed in its progress from speech to song, I have hitherto adhered rather closely to its *material* aspect. I have more prominently noted the changes assumed by it in its mechanical construction, and have considered its influence no further than to its first direct and physical effect. But I now propose to regard it with a more comprehensive gaze—to note the changes it assumes in relationship to the emotional circumstances with which it is connected, and to consider also the moral function it fulfils. In so doing, I think we shall find these new considerations will strengthen our impression of the truth and consistency of the former ones, and also reveal some remarkable and interesting truths connected with the subject.

At the outset of our considerations of the principle of Tone and Phrase in relationship to its attending sentiments, we are struck with one very remarkable peculiarity in this relationship, and it is the observation of this peculiarity that leads us to all our ensuing discoveries in the nature of the general subject of our inquiry.

In that species of language adopted by man as a medium for ordinary converse—that is particularly adapted for the imparting of what is substantial, positive, distinct, and definite; where the aspect of the principle in question is least prominently defined, where the effect of Rhythm is totally absent, and where the principle of Phrase itself is only partially and imperfectly indicated, we thus observe the above-mentioned peculiarity.

We find that the more conspicuous the indications of the principle of Phrase *do* appear,—the more the sentences are *balanced*,—the more intensely the influence of emphasis and pause exists therein —accent or fall; so, also the more *moral* and the less material—the more *comprehensive* and the less contracted—are the truths and circumstances represented, the more *emotional* and the less sensational are the sentiments expressed. Or, to describe this peculiarity as it naturally occurs; the more comprehensive and less contracted—the more moral and the less material—the more emotional and the less sensational—are the truths and sentiments to be imparted, the more does the speaker become impelled to avail himself, in conveying them, of the additional impressiveness that can be conferred upon this expression by the employment of the principle of Tone and Phrase, and thus the more conspicuous and the less imperfect in such cases do the exemplifications of this principle appear.

Proceeding to the more artistic forms of Prose, where the principle of Tone and Phrase does not occupy such a subordinate relationship with the truths and sentiments imparted, as in its preceding exemplifications in the language of ordinary converse; but where, on the other hand, we meet it much more conspicuously indicated, and where the impressions to be produced in the hearer seem to depend much more upon the *special action* of this principle than in the former circumstances, and whilst observing these changes in its aspect, noting also those changes that here present themselves, in its attending circumstances, we again meet with the before remarked peculiarity.

For in the language of the philosopher and the orator, in that of the public lecturer, the writer and the teacher, we observe that the circumstances and truths represented, and the sentiments expressed, are mostly such as are of an abstract, comprehensive, and emotional nature, and not such as are of a material, contracted, and sensational character. The arguments of such minds are based upon moral and comprehensive truths, not contracted and incidental ones;—upon emotions, not sensations, and so in further illustration of the peculiarity discovered in the previously considered exemplification of this principle, we here appropriately find a more conspicuous and elaborate employment of the principle of Tone and Phrase.

Proceeding onward to a still more artistic form of language, namely Poetry, we find that this species of language is still more remarkable in its representation of abstract and comprehensive circumstances and truths, and still less so in its representation of material and incidental ones—still more adapted for the expression of emotional impressions, and still less so for the expression of sensational ones, than other species of language; and so in continued illustration of the previously remarked peculiarity, we here again perceive that the principle in question is still more conspicuous, still further elaborated and developed, than in its before considered exemplifications.

It appears then that the sentence of ordinary converse, the speech of the Orator, the stanza of the Poet, are all more or less pervaded by this principle of Tone and Phrase; and that wherever in the whole range of utterance occupied by these mediums of expression, the truths and sentiments to be imparted are more or less comprehensive, or emotional—that there also is duly and inevitably found an appropriately increased or subdued effect of the principle of Tone and Phrase.

Now if we attentively consider this remarkable peculiarity, betrayed in the relationship of every exemplification of the principle of tone and phrase to those circumstances and truths, the representation of which such exemplification attends, and to those sentiments which it assists to express, we shall find that it admits of perfect explanation, and also that it brings us nearer to the perception of the subject of our next inquiry, namely, the *moral function* this principle fulfils.

It will be remembered that in the beginning of this Essay, when considering the general function fulfilled by this principle in the language of ordinary converse, it was remarked, "It is, how certain truths impress the individual alone, in distinction to how they may impress others, that the property in speech, of Tone, Emphasis, and Pause, particularly imparts." It will also be remembered that this conclusion was arrived at *from necessity:* that from the truth, there argued, that "the same fact existing in different minds may in each several case exist in a different phase; and thus be not exactly the same fact; and from the circumstance there pointed out, that "the ordinary symbols of speech are only calculated to represent the same fact according to two or three perceptions of it," that, therefore, a further and finer medium of expression—a medium more adaptive in representing the delicate distinctions in our perception of facts—*is required*, than the common and general materials of human speech." Now the conclusion that this requirement, this necessity, is supplied in the function of the principle of Tone and Phrase, though reasonable and extremely probable,—is, in the stage of the argument here alluded to, still *hypothetical.* But in the present stage of these considerations, that conclusion can be strengthened. And whilst endeavouring to establish it by the medium of recent observations, it will also be seen that this hypothesis sheds light in return upon these observations themselves.

For as, " wherever in the whole range of utterance occupied by speech, oratory, or poetry, the truths and sentiments to be imparted are, more or less comprehensive and emotional, there also is duly found an appropriately increased or subdued effect of the principle of Tone and Phrase." So it can be shown that wherever, in the whole range of utterance, the truths and sentiments are more or less comprehensive and emotional; that exactly there also they will be more *original,* more peculiar, to the narrator alone. This truth the reader will be conscious of himself, and I think will be disposed to allow ; however, it will now be further explored in proceeding to explain the lately considered peculiarity betrayed in the relationship of every exemplification of the principle of Tone and Phrase to those circumstances and truths, the representation of which such exemplification attends, and to those sentiments which it assists to express ; and here we shall perceive the hypothesis in the beginning of this Essay, throwing light upon the present considerations. It has been stated, then, that the sentence of ordinary converse, the speech of the orator, the stanza of the poet, are all more or less pervaded by the principle of Tone and Phrase, and that wherever, in the whole range of utterance, the truths and sentiments are more or less comprehensive and emotional, there, also, we inevitably find an appropriately increased or subdued effect of this principle,—we thus account for its consistency.

The reason of this circumstance, in the language of ordinary converse and in the speech of the orator, is apparent through the same argument that betrays the consistency of an elaborate exemplification of this principle attending the representation of circumstances, truths, and sentiments highly abstract, comprehensive, and emotional, as observed in meditative poetry.

For, the circumstances represented by the meditative poet being abstract circumstances—circumstances existing in the lofty and remote regions of the moral universe, thus impressing their nature but rarely upon the general appreciation of man, and only discerned in the wide sensitiveness of poetical meditation. And the truths represented both in meditative poetry and the artistic forms of prose being moral and comprehensive truths—

truths of principle betrayed in the action of a multitude of material and incidental truths—
    "All suffering doth destroy or is destroyed,"
it will be perceived that the discovery of such circumstances and truths involves in the regarder a wide and sustained exertion of the appreciative faculties, and a *great effort of imagination*, and that the impression eventually produced within him by the above original discovery must be an *original impression*.

Now such an impression as the above being peculiar to the imparter alone, it is evident that it cannot be conveyed to others by an appeal to their experience; and as the particular form of influence that aroused it exists not only in the consciousness of one mind alone, but, even to exist here involves a particular series of considerations and a peculiar temper of imagination, it will also be perceived that this influence *cannot undergo perfect representation*, owing partly to the difficulty of obtaining amongst the materials of ordinary human speech, symbols of expression sufficiently correct to duly suggest the exact balance of considerations that reveal it; but principally to the impossibility of conveying, by any but its especial medium of expression—that indefinite but essential spiritual tone of the breast—

that new and spontaneous expanse of imagination, in the prophetic warmth of which those considerations started into life and in whose mystic light they became developed.

The above influence then not admitting of perfect representation, the impression produced by it cannot be imparted by means of a repetition, in others of a similar process as previously occurred in the imparter, because the representation of the original influence being imperfect, the effect of this representation must be imperfect also, and thus the above-mentioned process would be in such an instance but partially repeated. Consequently in endeavouring to convey such impressions as the above by the principle of representation,—in the description of circumstances and truths of an *abstract, elevated, moral,* and *comprehensive* character—in the expression of sentiments accruing from their contemplation, it is obvious that for the due interpretation of the speaker, and for the appropriate impression of the listener, the employment of some other principle *besides that of representation* is necessary and indispensable, *to kindle within the listener an effort of imagination and glow of spirit*, of a kindred nature to that within the imparter, in the warmth of which he became conscious of the emotions he is conveying.

Now in the necessity we thus discover upon these occasions, for the employment of some other principle besides that of representation, and in the regular presence upon such occasions of appropriately elaborate and conspicuous exemplifications of the principle of Tone and Phrase, we are enabled to perceive the moral function this principle fulfils. We are enabled to perceive that this function is to further in ordinary language the expression and conveyance of common emotion, and in the higher forms of language, to attend and even assist in an elaborate and conspicuous degree, the *embodiment* of elevated and comprehensive truths, and thus become the chief medium for the expression of particular and original emotion.

A few paragraphs back, I alluded (amongst the circumstances attending the birth of an impression derived from the contemplation of a comprehensive truth) to a " sustained exertion of the appreciative faculties and a great effort of imagination ;" to an " indefinite but essential spiritual tone of the breast—anew and spontaneous expanse of imagination," and following this train of thought, I now endeavour to throw light upon that *inward process* by means of which the principle in question possesses the remarkable property of aiding mental perception, and inspiring emotional expression.

This inward process is first perceived in considering the remarkable influence of the Principle of Tone and Phrase upon the faculty termed " Imagination"—of its instantaneous production of a vague grandeur, a high expectancy within the breast, which under its influence seems to swell into a boundless temple of conception; bright, warm, and vivid; ripe and expanding for the embodiment of sublime and lofty imagery.

Here then, in the communication of a great and comprehensive truth, and in the expression of the emotion it has aroused—we are enabled to perceive that this process, this function of the principle of Tone and Phrase, consists of the *imparting of that indefinite glow of spirit, that mystic and prophetic inspiration of imagination,* in the warmth of which a presage of the above truth became vaguely conceived, invoking to life and sustaining in their progress those series of considerations which led to its full revelation. We are enabled to perceive the creating of an ardent expectancy within the breast, where the mental perception and moral sympathy are vaguely straining for action, and, in a state of intense susceptibility, awaiting the suggestions of the principle of representation, for the spontaneous production within the listener of the full idea and exact emotion that first impelled the original conceiver to avail himself, for expression, of the particular eloquence of the principle of Tone and Phrase.

Thus the remarkable process by which this principle imbues others with emotion, is to *kindle the imagination*, thus to *vivify and heighten the mental perception*, and thus *to warm and deepen the moral sympathy*. Its peculiar effect is to invoke an extension of the mental perception and moral sympathy from their common and instinctive sphere, where all that excites their action is the material circumstances and truths which we become conscious of through the external senses, to the realms of imagination, where that which calls forth their exercise lies in the spiritual and infinite expanse of abstract and lofty circumstances, and of moral and comprehensive truths.

Through the preceding considerations we are enabled to perceive some interesting particulars in the nature of language itself. We see that in all those cases in which it attains to the effect of accent and fall, emphasis and pause, and exemplifies conspicuously the principle of Tone and Phrase, it is the embodiment of abstract and lofty circumstances, of comprehensive truths, and of high and original sentiments. It is the influence which aids the *expression* of such imagery and emotion by the speaker, and at the same time, that which furthers the *impression* of the same in taking place within the hearer. It is, then, the *relief* of an expanded imagination, of an extended appreciation and of an enlarged sympathy in the utterer, and, at the same time, in the wise contrivance of nature, the *kindler* of such fulness of moral existence within the listener.

We are thus enabled to discern rather more deeply than usual into the inward nature of that climax of the elements of human speech termed " Eloquence." We see how it is constituted and what is its office. We see that it arises in that elaborate exemplification of the principle of Tone and Phrase which the speaker is impelled in the contemplation of lofty and abstract circumstances, and of comprehensive truths, to *avail* himself of, to relieve the pressure of original sentiments, conceived by a mental appreciation and moral sympathy extended and enlarged into the imagination; and that it is that influence which he is necessitated to *employ* in order to create such extended and enlarged condition of the appreciative capacity—to kindle such sentiments—in the breast of the listener.

And although this elaborate exemplification of the principle in question, in the appeal of the orator, in the dignified forms of Prose, in animated

speeches, in assertions of honour, and in defences
of life, may appear to accompany the representation
of contracted truths, and of the ordinary sentiments of humanity; still, it will generally be found,
that it is not these incidental truths and ordinary
sentiments, relating immediately to the particular
case, that kindles the advanced exemplification of
the principle of Tone and Phrase, but those more
abstract, comprehensive and original circumstances,
truths and sentiments which the former ones
suggest. In the imparting of an incidental truth,
and of an ordinary sentiment, these will be
found to arouse full and appropriate perceptions
and emotions, through the action of their bare
and unassisted representation upon the mental
perception in its simple capacity, and upon the
moral sympathy in its instinctive sphere. But
where the circumstances, truths, and sentiments,
that are being imparted, suggest the existence of
other abstract and *lofty* circumstances, *great* and
comprehensive truths, and the conception of *original*
sentiments; it will be found that it is in the imparting of this latter imagery and emotion whence
arises the striking Emphasis and the effective Pause.
It is these which inspire the rapture of eloquence,
the enthusiasm of enunciation, the " utterance and
the power of speech" in the speaker, and, to be

duly appreciated, demand the *influence of the same* upon the hearer.

> "What we will do we do upon command,
> And He that hath commanded is the King."
>
> ——Erroneous vassal! the great *King of Kings*
> Hath in the table of His law commanded
> That *thou shalt do no murder!*

Again,

> * * * "From the high host
> Of stars, to the lulled lake and mountain coast,
> *All is concentr'd in a life intense.*
> Where not a beam, nor air, nor leaf is lost
> But hath a part of being, and *a sense
> Of that which is of all Creator and defence.*"

The italics define the passages where the Poet has risen to the perception of a *comprehensive truth* and in which the utterer retires more completely from the consciousness of what is around him into the solitude of his imagination, and thus by his manner of enunciation, his Tone, Emphasis, and Pause, renders sensitive and expands the imaginative capacity of his hearers.

Thus the laws of human appreciation may be compared to a certain extent, to those of occular vision; for, as the star that lies removed and far from the complete scrutiny of the eye, occupying a loftier position, and commanding a more comprehensive influence in the universe than other objects, requires the conspicuous apparatus of the astronomer—in order that its appropriately brilliant reflections of light may shine upon the eye; so does the sublime, beautiful, elevated and comprehensive truth, lying far beyond the unassisted scrutiny of the human mind and from the instinctive sympathy of the human heart, require a more conspicuous and elaborate apparatus of expression in arousing its appropriate emotions in the listener's breast.

In the course of the preceding considerations the reflection is suggested, of how great is the importance of the imaginative faculty in the discovery of new truths of a moral nature, if not of those of any other character.

For useful, elevated, and glorious as is the faculty of *pure intellect*, it is still not to this alone that we are indebted for all the triumphs of the human mind. As I have before remarked in describing the inward process through which a new truth becomes revealed, there rises in the first place within the breast, a primary warmth, a vague grandeur of feeling, a prophetic glow and mystic halo of imagination, amidst which the new truth becomes hugely and indefinitely revealed. Such is the condition of the breast in the attainment of a new discovery *ere the faculty of reason has been once consciously put in action.*

Now it is this vague presence of a new figure within the vapoury and twilight realm of imagination, it is this undefined discovery brooding upon the consciousness that first incites the reasoning faculty to action—that suggests amidst the vast and unexplored space of speculation, the general direction for thought to pursue,—that in its mystery provokes, and as it becomes more lucid, sustains the ardour of the mind until its connexion with known truths is traced and its existence thus confirmed.

The term Imagination is generally received as the name for a faculty of the breast of a very indefinite character. In the sense in which it is ordinarily applied and understood, it means an action of the mind very grand and gorgeous, but still useless and unpractical. But in its true sense it is, metaphorically speaking, the moral universe in which the intellectual system exists.

It is the spiritual glow and moral radiance of this faculty, that defines the celestial concave of the mind, as the sun defines that of the physical universe, without which the operations of reason could attain to no further result than could those of nature without the warm and luminous concave of heaven.

In its literal sense imagination is the faculty to sustain imagery within the mind, to suspend scenes, circumstances, and truths simultaneously before the attention that their correct relationship and complete nature may become revealed in a wide embrace of the reason; thus he in whom it exists largely surveys in his mental glance a wider track of what is known, and is thus guided to perceive further into the regions beyond than others whose capacity of imagination is less. By possessing the faculty of sustaining a considerable number of known truths in his mind, he is enabled to see their *correct relationship* and their more *complete nature,* and is thus guided to perceive their onward connection with others. Now it is the perception of this *onward continuation of truth* that constitutes an action of imagination in its higher sense, and as it has been shown in the above remarks that the discernment of this onward continuation of truth results solely from a previous and simultaneous realization in the mind of a considerable portion of visible truth, it will now be perceived that it is only through the possession of imagination in its literal sense, whence accrues the possession of that faculty in its more advanced meaning. It will now be perceived that it is only through the previously described innate power of embracing, in one broad mental survey, the visible array of physical or moral truths (relating respectively to certain departments of physical or moral inquiry) that the complete nature, power, and effect of such truths is observed.

Here we also perceive the reason why the possession of the imaginative faculty is always attended by a manifestation of *enthusiasm,* for when a person possessing largely the capacity of imagination manifests simultaneously an intense enthusiasm, it is not because he views the objects of his contemplation more *extravagantly* than others, but more *correctly;* not because they glow before his vision in colours falsely bright, but truly bright. It is (in his comprehensive glance) the revelation of physical or moral truths in their complete nature and full power that incites the rapture and enthusiasm of his breast; and, as I have before remarked, it is only through perceiving the complete nature of known truths (and in the vividness and enthusiasm of mind accruing from the above perception) that the figure of a *new* and *onward truth* is discerned, dimly defined in the cloudy haze of speculation; the perception of this latter phenomenon constituting an action of imagination in its higher sense, when

> "Into that darkness   *   *   *
> By some prophetic feeling taught
> We launch the bold adventurous thought."

These observations are not meant to imply that the conception of a new truth by the faculty of imagination is clearly identical with the inference of the existence of a new truth by the faculty of reason, but that true conceptions of imagination are always in *the track of reason;* that however vaguely they are defined—however wild and mysterious their aspect may at first appear—they always *lie off the coast of truth.*

Such being the circumstances that attend the remarkable and prophetic conceptions of imagination, it will now be perceived that these conceptions may be accounted for as the result of a *latent extension of the intellect*—of an involuntary onward spring of the reason to a new and distant conclusion, the considerations of the intermediate space having occurred so rapidly and unconsciously as to render the result like inspiration. But whether the conceptions of imagination be the result of Reason, Genius, Inspiration, or any unknown influence, if they are really conceptions of imagination—that is, of imagination in its full and true application which includes both its literal and prophetic sense, and not in that in which it signifies an unnatural and desultory wandering of mind—they always reveal themselves in the van of reason, and in most cases, by the onward march of that faculty, admit of becoming confirmed as true inspirations. Of this character are the imaginative conceptions of all great minds—poetic or scientific, appearing respectively, as they become divested of their primary mystery before the approaching light of reason, in the form of new moral, or physical, truths.

Thus the great imaginative capacity, as described in these remarks, being, as I have previously explained, that feature of moral organization which is *essential* to all original intellects, is appropriate with such an assumption also found to be *common* to these; this latter circumstance of its existence accounting for that *general* broadness of glance and *kindred* elevation of sentiment which inevitably prevails amongst the truly great.

In making a period to these considerations regarding the nature of Imagination, let it be once more observed, that although the possession of this capacity in the first place depends upon, and proceeds from, an innate and divine warmth of spirit, glowing in the sacred mysteries of our being, even as the availability-for-life of the celestial concave of nature, proceeds from the sun; that still the production within the above capacity of a subsequent result (whether this result first betrays itself in the immediate van of reason, or far in advance, hovering remotely in the dim and unrelieved space of the unknown) is always *preceded* by an extensive operation of the other faculties of the mind; even as the production of the shrub upon the face of the earth—though wrought by the influence of the sun—still is always *preceded* by the operations of nature at its root; the plant being only visible to the eye—the *immediate cause* of its production being hidden—even as the result of imagination is alone revealed, whilst the *immediate process of reason* that led to it is latent. For the conceptions of true imagination may, in illustration of their nature, be compared to the results of the universe, and as there are many of the latter that, beholding with our sense, we cannot account for by our reason, to which nevertheless, we can nearly follow the action of the physical laws that produced them, and thus discover that they still lie within the *path* of natural law; so all conceptions of the mind that beheld in imagination are not yet established by reason (if they are true imaginative conceptions) may still be nearly confirmed by pursuing the path of reason; for it is above this path in its invisible course into the unknown, that all true-born imaginative conceptions alone and assuredly arise, even as it is alone within the definite, prescribed, but *invisible orbit* of physical law where the stars above us shine, though apparently unlocated in the vague and infinite space of Heaven.

These considerations upon the Imagination have been entered into from a desire to define clearly the true nature of that capacity—to suggest the indispensable conditions of its possession, and to point out those peculiar moral circumstances amidst which its conceptions can alone arise. That a true exposition of the circumstances of its existence, of its greatest development always existing sympathetically with the broadest capacities of intellect, and its highest conceptions always revealing themselves, not beside, but in front of the path of reason—may impel those who aspire to the possession or attainment of this great and glorious faculty, to seek it in the study of the *rational*, and amidst the glowing realms of nature; and not to countenance, as a visitation of imagination, that desultory abstraction, which is only present where intellect is idle, lethargic, or totally absent; whose sphere instead of verging upon that of reason, is wholly removed from the plane of the rational, and whose conceptions—ridiculous, not sublime, lurid, not lovely, deformities to the healthy and natural eye of taste, because inconsistent with nature,—instead of revealing themselves in the path of reason, can never arise save where reason has fallen; instead of invoking and stimulating the ardour of intellect, can only deaden and confound it; and instead of becoming confirmed and clear in the light of approaching intelligence, are assuredly there dispelled.

There prevails, however, at present throughout the whole field of Art where the faculty of imagination is mainly the productive influence, an immense conceit—the conceit of *mysticism*. This is especially visible in modern poetry, and literature generally. There are many modern allegorical poems (the sole purpose of which is the elucidation of mystery, the laying bare of the pure thread of truth from the web of circumstances and the separate and clear embodiment of it under familiar forms) upon whose forehead nevertheless "mystery" is imperviously written; the moral of which was inscrutable upon the day of publication, and is at the present moment equally in advance of the intelligence of the age. In which, though there exist colours, figures, light and shade, constructive skill, expression, power, and probably genius, these but constitute the

"Throne of the Invisible,"

for in the midst of all, there yawns that pressing want,—meaning; that first necessity that in aught prepared for the mind and to enter in the mind of man, must pervail,—intelligible idea.

In general literature again, this tendency to veer, not into those pregnant clouds tinged by the sun of reason, but into the wholly insulated obscure of space, equally prevails. For here we meet, also, with vague appeals to the imagination—the habit of indifinite allusion—the way of verging, artistically, upon the obscure. This is certainly sometimes accompanied with an announcement— the announcement of some simple and long-known truth, yet all is expressed in the assumption of such an elevated confidence of manner, and in a style so impressive, as seems only consistent with the matter being highly original, or totally infallible.

Now in all these conceptions, the only attributes common with those of true imaginative representations are the attributes of mystery, incoherency, and that of being apparently disjoined from the visible system of Nature.

> "Yet there are things whose strong reality
> Outshines our fairy land; in shape and hues
> More beautiful than our fantastic sky."

There is a mystery of truth as well as a mystery of error; there may be conceptions soaring *above* visible Nature, as well as conceptions sinking beneath it.

There is doubtless a charm attending the mysterious, but this charm solely consists in the consciousness of the existence of some great and brilliant truth enshrouded therein. To those who love to be mystified, and it seems from the success which has attended this style of Art, that to thousands this process is not disagreeable, I say, confront the mystery of Truth! met in the paths of reason, and beheld over the plains of Nature.

To those whose mind loves to wander in regions out of this visible system of Nature, I say, let it not wander below, but guide it by the light of intellect to the shining regions beyond! Let it not ignobly revel in its own false, shadowy, and abortive creations; but anticipate the discoveries of reason in the unexplored works of God, bodily or spiritual; for amidst them assuredly it can alone find its true sphere of action, and appropriate subjects for contemplation. In them alone can it meet with that which will truly nourish, expand, and elevate it; in them alone can it confront the greatest wonders; and amidst them only can it survey the highest wisdom and worth.

The principle of Tone and Phrase has now been traced from its exemplifications in ordinary speech to those betrayed by it in the highest forms that human language can assume. In pursuing the progress of this principle we have now arrived at the confines of that precise and objective medium of expression appropriate for the practical intercommunication of man. Yet the principle under consideration is still in a progressive condition, for as the human voice concludes its palpable burden and falls overcharged by that feeling, it cannot all convey, then, this principle of Tone and Phrase, "takes up the wondrous tale," and clothed in Angel garb, emerges from the mortal form of speech its Heavenly and immortal spirit—"Music."

It has been observed in considering the process by which the principle of Tone and Phrase, as exemplified in conjunction with language, relieves the expression and assists the conveyance of emotion; that an obvious part of this process is the rendering of the imagination of the listener susceptible to the realization of those circumstances, the definite aspect of which is embodied in the attending language, it is thus the extending his appreciation and enlarging his sympathy to the influence of this scenery in his imagination.

It will be perceived, then, that in thus imparting emotions, the original circumstances and truths, the original *influences*, must to a certain extent, be reproduced before the listener, either by description or representation; and that as the function fulfilled by the principle of Tone and Phrase, is to render the listener's imagination *susceptible* to those influences, — in these circumstances, this principle imparts emotion in an *auxiliary* capacity and *indirectly*.

But in music the exemplifications of the principle of Tone and Phrase are attended by no representation, by no description. In becoming emotionally impressed by music we are not assisted by the action of our appreciation or sympathy upon any imbodied influences. We receive the impressions *direct* from the composer, through the influence of the principle of Tone and Phrase *alone*, with function undivided, which principle now leaps to its zenith of development, to its fullest and most perfect exemplifications, and to its greatest effects.

But from the previous considerations into the nature of the different exemplifications of the principle in question we inferred that the impressions derived from the contemplation of the more lofty and comprehensive circumstances and truths found expression and interpretation in the more advanced exemplifications of the principle of Tone and Phrase, which phenomenon seems to imply that in the present case the exemplifications of this principle being of the highest order they must therefore constitute the expression of the highest and most comprehensive character of emotion.

Now this assumption is not only thus shown to be consistent, from the fact of the principle of Tone and Phrase being in its exemplification in Music, in the most advanced development, but may also be further supported by that other remarkable peculiarity of the principle in question as exemplified in Music—namely, of its constituting in these circumstances the *sole function* of imbuing emotion—of its possessing, in this stage of its progress, the remarkable property of conveying emotion *direct* to the breast of the listener.

For it can be demonstrated* how music—through being independent of the conjunctive conveyance of the influences of these emotions as they appeared in nature, but being on the other hand of a nature so subtle and ethereal as to conduct such emotions *direct* to the breasts of others:—thereby possesses the original property of conveying *impressions aroused by influences of a different character, simultaneously*, which cannot be accomplished by any medium of expression that involves, in conveying emotions, the necessity of the conjunctive conveyance of the original influences of those emotions, because these influences being, in such circumstances, of a *different* character—their *simultaneous* description or representation would be totally inconsistent with physical law and natural propriety.

Now, as we thus behold in music a medium appropriate for the simultaneous expression of emotions of a different character, that is, of emotions that were derived from influences of a varied nature, and which, though aroused *successively*, as the influences in nature that created them, became opposite to the contemplation of their possessor, nevertheless are imparted

* See Essay on "The Relationship of Music to the other Fine Arts."

simultaneously, and not only imparted simultaneously, but in a higher temper and more perfect condition through this simultaneous conveyance; that is, corrected and extended by the judgment, deepened and vivified by contrast:—we are again supported in the assumption that in music there exists a medium for the expression of the highest and most comprehensive character of emotions;—when

" Stirs the feeling infinite."

I have now arrived at the principal period in the subject of these inquiries, and to which I pointed at the opening of this essay. Having now traced the progress of the principle of Tone and Phrase from its " first faint indications in human speech to its kingly and overpowering effects in Music," and I now proceed in conformity with the subsequent announcement, to continue " to account for many of those remarkable effects of the after fullness and maturity of this principle, in Music."

Pursuing then the consideration of the comprehensive nature of the musical medium of expression, it will be seen that it is this wideness and vagueness in the character of the impressions which the composer relieves himself of through the medium of Music, which explains that remarkable and hitherto unillumined peculiarity in the effect of this influence—namely, the same piece producing different impressions on each listener.

Now it is not intended to accomplish the extraordinary psychological feat of tracing the impressions of the composer through the inscrutable mysteries of musical effect to their resurrection in the listener, but it must be remembered that there is a certain law of harmony and propriety established by nature, which enjoins the same *medium of expression* which we are naturally impelled to adopt in relieving ourselves of emotion, to be at the same time the appropriate *influence* for inspiring the same emotion in others. And thus it can be argued that the perception of the peculiar appropriateness of Music as a medium for relieving impressions of an *inclusive* character in the composer, explains its remarkable property of inspiring *different emotions* in each listener.

In explaining further the meaning of the effect of Music, let the reader's attention be referred to the fact previously endeavoured to be established, that " Music" is the highest exemplification of that principle of Tone and Phrase of which we discover the existence in ordinary human speech, and that this principle in itself is the only *direct, original, and unalloyed language of human emotions*. Of all the external evidences of inward emotion that our senses can become conscious of, the effect of this principle is the external evidence *most closely and immediately connected with the emotions themselves,* and whenever we become imbued with an impression by *its influence alone,* we receive this impression in the *most direct* manner that is possible. For, as has been before observed, when an emotion is imparted by describing, representing, or reproducing in some way the natural influence that first aroused it, then such an emotion is conveyed by means of a repetition, in the listener, of that process which previously occurred in the speaker; but when an emotion is imparted through the *sole medium* of the principle of Tone and Phrase, it is then conveyed by *direct* and unalloyed communication.

It must be remembered then that the principle of "Music," from its faintest to its fullest development, is of an emotional nature throughout; and also that to impart a grand and comprehensive inward impression, kindled by the successive contemplation of influences of a varied nature, is not only *to convey the feelings of the utterer,* but also *to express those of the listener,* who, in such cases is thus not only becoming duly conscious of the emotions of others, but is also expressing his own.

This consideration, then, still further explains the meaning of the effect of music upon us, for it accounts for that remarkable condition of the breast produced by the influence of music, which involves the rapture of reception with the relief of expression. It accounts for that wonderful property of sublime compositions that are of whatever emotions their eloquence has produced, at once the inspiration and relief.

It must be borne in mind that, in treating Music as that high medium to which alone it is given to impart these comprehensive and inclusive impressions, and to create these broad effects, I am treating of it in its most elevated forms and grandest phases, and not in those ordinary aspects in which it is, as is most frequently the case, the exponent and expression of some particular, distinct and positive sentiment. Its capability for assuming expression of a distinctive character exists quite consistently with that grander endowment of its nature which has been more dwelt upon in these pages,—of infinite depth, sublimity, and comprehensiveness of effect; only to perceive or explain the latter phenomenon requires the whole line of argument,—the whole body of considerations contained in this inquiry, to be kept steadily in view, whilst to account for the former, it is but necessary to bear in mind the simple consideration of the emotional origin of Music.

It is also this consideration of the thoroughly emotional nature and constitution of music that explains its remarkable and infinite *variety* of expression—an expression that can assume characters as directly opposite, as minutely distinctive, and as generally varied as the endlessly changeful aspects assumed by human emotion itself;—an expression that can assume a character, gay, cheerful, or pensive; sad, sorrowful, or passionate; fervent, pious, religious, or solemn; severe, grand, or sublime, with a peculiar faithfulness and facility, with such a natural truth and ease as unmistakably betrays the purely emotional origin of the influence of music in those simple, beautiful, and expressive exemplifications of tone, accent, and fall, which we perceive in ordinary speech.

But amidst all this variety in the character of expression that music admits of, amidst all the different orders of human emotions whose aspects the stream of music so clearly reflects, it is deeply urgent to remark one order of emotions which the influence of music represents with most wonderful vividness and eloquence of interpretation, and with most remarkable pathos and grandeur of effect, that is "religious emotion."

It must be felt by all who consider what they feel that the exalted temperament of the human feelings, kindled by the great and momentous influence of Religion, is echoed in the effects of music so eloquently, purely, faithfully, and worthily, as to leave all other mediums of emotional expression far behind. Painting can express so much of the character of religious emotion as can visibly appear in the aspect of the human countenance. Language can point out its presence by narrating those virtuous actions which it impels—it can signify where it resides by depicting all its amiable indications in the outward motions of life. Yes, language can point out, amidst all the varied ways that are so thickly ramified throughout this human plain, those paths where religious emotion passed over, and can show the brightness in which they shine and the glory in which they end. Words can represent the feelings of those with religious emotions in the action of such feelings upon the outward world, but the subtle emotion itself, in its great seat of existence within the human heart, in the deep rapture and sublimity of feeling attending its possession, they cannot, they *need* not express. Of all the different classes of sentiments that, kindled by the varied influences of life, become grafted in the heart of man, there is not one that when once planted, roots itself so deeply, largely, and abidingly as the religious order of impressions. There are no impressions that press so strongly upon the confines of the human breast that contains them,— that imbue so forcibly their possessor with the disparity between the boundlessness, might, and eternity of their own nature, and that of the narrow, frail, and brief tenement that holds them.

In proceeding to account as briefly as possible for the peculiar effects that distinguish sacred music, for the individuality, chastened beauty, and deep sublimity of character that it ever sustains, it will be of assistance to cursorily consider the distinctions that exist between the character of worldly, and of religious emotions, and this can be shown by considering individually a few particular emotions—for instance, joy, gratitude, and hope.

That breast is not cold nor unreplete that swells with any of the above feelings when of a worldly nature: but what is the fervour and fulness of such a breast to that which confines these emotions, when kindled by the inspiration of religious truth!

The emotion of worldly joy is frail and uncertain, of limited life, and liable to be dispelled and swept away by the first breath that wanders from the ever-surrounding presence of adversity. The emotion of joy inspired by Religion, on the other hand, possesses that greatest of all characteristics, it is *abiding;* so much so that what deteriorates from the continuance of the former character of the emotion is conducive to the existence of this; the same influence which is the death of the former, is the life of the latter. For adversity that *dispels* joy of a worldly nature, *confirms* it when of a religious character.

Again, the joy produced by the most favourable conjunction of circumstances is tame and but a negative emotion compared to that produced by the influence of Religion, even when amidst a conjunction of worldly circumstances the most unfortunate; for here the feeling is not tame, but enthusiastic; not a *negative* emotion, but a *positive* one; not implying a state of the breast amiable, and free from the reproach of conscience, but, on the other hand, implying a condition of nature sublime, and aspiring to divine righteousness.

The great distinction between worldly and religious gratitude is so obvious and palpable as almost to require no exemplification. For what breast that is at all conscious of the favours bestowed by God, will not be understood to entertain an emotion of gratitude, when inspired by such favours, far different than when kindled by the advantages that can possibly be bestowed by man? What other character of this emotion of gratitude can approach in intensity, fervour, and expansiveness of existence, that which rebounds from the consideration that all health, joy, and happiness, and the genial and beautiful natural laws upon which such blessings rest, we owe to our Maker? That the adaptation of the whole universe itself to satisfy our wants, to gladden our sense, to kindle our affections, to call forth rapture in our hearts, and to elevate and expand our minds, we owe to the intentional act of the Creator,—that we not only owe, ourselves, our present blessings and future inheritance to his *making*, but to his previous *conceiving?*—that we, with our joys, are not only the *work* of His hands, but also the *conception* of His mind. The well-known injunction, "Praise the Lord," is simple and common, but it is also deeply wise and consistent. For the result of generations, of the widest human experience and the profoundest mental consideration, resolves itself into a boundless emotion of the breast which, than the above, can assume no more consistent verbal expression.

How different, too—how much more enduring and steadfast is the emotion of hope inspired by religious, compared to that kindled by worldly, promises.

For worldly hope may wane through disappointment or expire through fulfilment. But religious hope, when once lit in the heart, neither wanes through disappointment nor in this life can expire in fulfilment, but throughout all circumstances continues to burn ever steadily and brightly to the end of its course. Again, how much more earnest and intense must this feeling be when of a religious than when of a worldly character; for how can such ills and sorrows that can possibly be changed by the fulfilment of any worldly hope, be so bitter and serious as those that can alone be relieved by the great consolation of Religion? How deep is that dark wound, rent by death in the human heart, that Religion alone can heal? How soon, in reviewing the numerous evils of life, with the view of alleviating, do we find that all earthly hope is vain and powerless? How soon do we meet with those sorrows to which the hope, reliance, and trust in Divine justice, mercy, and all watchfulness, can alone impart consolation and comfort? Consequently how much the more precious and dear to humanity, beyond all others, must be this holy star of Religious Hope, insomuch that it shines upon evils so dark that nothing else can illumine.

These considerations have been entered into to

refer the reader's attention to the remarkable distinction between feeling of an ordinary, and of a religious character,—to call to mind certain qualities in the latter, quite beyond the nature of the former,—to show that whereas emotions of an ordinary character are entertained in abeyance to the condition and circumstances of this life, those of a religious nature are entertained totally independent of them, and only subjective to conditions and circumstances far more stupendous, and that are eternal; to point out that whereas it is in the nature of all worldly feelings to suffer interruption, to decline, and to end; it is the abiding character of religious emotions to suffer no interruption, to endure throughout all influences, and to continually augment; and thus to impress the reader with the remarkable steadfastness, intensity, and firmness of character that must distinguish these feelings, and with the altogether sublime and solemn condition of that breast which is charged with the fervent and momentous inspiration of religious emotion.

It will be remembered that in some previous considerations we discovered that the appropiate position of the principle of Tone and Phrase, is, in the representation of circumstances, truths, and sentiments, of a lofty, comprehensive, and original character,—that its moral function is to relieve the breast of emotions acquired by the contemplation of the above order of influences, that is, by the extension of the appreciative faculties, and the enlargement of the sympathy; and also to create that primary warmth, expansiveness, and ripeness of imagination in the listener, appropriate for the embodiment of the above imagery, and thus to aid that extension of appreciation and enlargement of sympathy in him, which is essential for his becoming duly impressed.

In proceeding, then, with the endeavour to account for the remarkable adequacy, efficiency, and eloquence with which "music" lends itself to the expression of sacred feelings,—for the readiness, facility, and general tendency it manifests to abstract its voice from the utterance of all other impressions, and to upraise it, in hallowed breathings or celestial echoes, to the awful expression of religious emotion, it must be next considered whether the influences that arouse religious feelings are such as demand, in so doing, an expansion of imagination, an extension of the appreciative faculties, and an enlargement of the sympathy.

In entering into this consideration it will be at once perceived that the religious influences of emotion, are such as demand, in duly impressing us, an exertion of imagination of the highest and widest degree. It will be clearly observed that religious truths, religious injunctions, religious promises, require a most exalted effort of the imagination before their appropriate emotions are kindled within us. Thus, in becoming conscious of those Heavenly emotions that accrue from the consideration of the wise, mild, and amiable injunctions of religion, our imagination first pictures the bright and happy condition of humanity, the virtuous and admirable examples that the fulfilment of these injunctions would inevitably produce; in comparison to that mixed joy and dubious happiness, and to those mingled examples of generosity and selfishness which is the highest result of purely natural injunctions:—our imagination then first pictures what should be the results of religious injunctions, which, thus warmly embodied, kindle the glow of our sympathy and inspire appropriate emotion.

By the same process do we become conscious of that fervent and deep emotion of consolation that accompanies the consideration of religious promises. For does not the imagination, in the first place, throw its light and colours forward in the breast to the fulfilment of our great coming heritage, until we realize in the mind our deliverance from death to eternal life—the restoration to us of those we have lost—the forgiveness of our sins—the satisfactory exposure, by the light of Divine justice, of those of our actions that its earthly administration left in dubiety and darkness. Is it not then by the rapid delineation of this momentous scene in the imagination that our sympathies are awakened in their intensest life, kindling simultaneously the high and appropriate emotion of our hearts.

We see, then, that all moral truths of a Religious character involve, for due appreciation, a considerable effort of the imagination, and it will be hereafter shewn that a similar exertion of the imaginative faculty is also required for appropriately realising in the mind all those religious truths that are of a circumstantial character.

But there is a great distinction between the nature of the effort of imagination made in the conception of religious influences, and the nature of that put forth in the conception of all others that require the exertion of the imaginative faculty.

The effort of imagination, wrought under the influence of religious truth, is one on a totally different and larger scale than can be kindled by any other influence. For, it will be perceived, that all other influences—all natural truths, however comprehensive, however far and magnificent, invoking howsoever great an exertion of imagination to bring them within reach of the moral sympathy or mental appreciation, — still require the creative faculty to delineate no picture within the mind but such a one as is *consistent with the natural conditions of the universe* in which we exist, in conformity with which the character and powers of our respective faculties were designed. Whereas influences of a religious character demand for due emotional appreciation such a totally strange, grand, and *unearthly flight* of imagination—they demand the delineation of such a supernatural and stupendous picture in the mind, as imagination could never have found in all the dignified space of natural morality for desirability; nor within the vast starry depths of the material Universe for circumstantial magnificence.

Commensurate with the superior greatness of the effort of imagination, exerted in the reception of religious—over that put forth in receiving impressions from all other, influences, is also the superior fervency and earnestness of the response of the *sympathy* and *appreciation* to this appeal, over the sympathetic and appreciative responses to all other imaginative representations. For what other immediate influences of emotion, embodied in the mind, or existing palpably before us, can kindle our sympathy so strongly and earnestly as those which religious truth involves even when pictured only in imagination?

What can be more calculated to excite the strongest sympathy of mankind than the realization, though only within the mind, of the promises, injunctions, and truths of religion? The deliverance from the ghastly oblivion of the grave—the inheritance of eternal life—the re-union of those long lost to us in the mystery of Death—the bright reward of patient endurance—the exposure of concealed guilt to the all-searching light of Divine truth—the meeting with the Creator in the aspect of an Almighty Father who has ever watched over us, remembering our temptations, and forgiving us our sins—the complete triumph of Justice, and the everlasting exaltation of Virtue. What other scenery, wrought in the prophetic light of imagination, can inspire *such sympathy* as this? What Picture, even glowing within the frame of actual life and reality and grouped upon the tide of time, can arouse human interest and sympathy so fervent as does this? though delineated only in the etherial creation of the mind; but invoked by the voice of God, and tinged with the colors of conscience.

As has been previously hinted, it can also be shown how superior an effort of imagination, and how much greater a task for the appreciation, must be wrought, in order for us to become duly impressed by *circumstantial* truths, when these are of a religious nature than when of any other character.

For though many circumstantial influences of a natural character demand in duly impressing us an exertion of the imaginative faculty, in order that the appreciation may form some analogy between them and the circumstantial influences immediately before us; still it will be observed that such influences never demand an effort of imagination extending beyond the bounds, and incompatible with the design, of the Physical Universe, and that might not possibly be superseded by the guidance of intellect.

But what mental pilots have navigated so far into the sea of truth as to lead our minds to a due perception of Heavenly circumstance? What wondrous standard has yet been compiled from which we can take out the mighty proportions of Divine state? On what refulgent prism shall we cast our eyes to see the glowing colours, wherein to enrobe our ideas of celestial splendour? What beacons of human intellect have been erected past the confines of this natural sphere, across that vast and mystic sea that stretches from the port of Death, and rolls beyond the shores of Time, to guide the appreciation of man to compass the circumstantial wonders—the scenic glories—that majestically attend the existence of Religious Truth?

Therefore, in forming our idea of these things —for we must form some idea of them to become emotionally impressed—in becoming possessed of feelings appropriate from the consideration of religious circumstance, how slightly we are assisted by our intellect, and how greatly we must exert the imagination! How ever soaring and straining upon the extreme verge of its sphere must the creative faculty be, in performing its part of that inward process by which we become conscious of emotions inspired by religious influences; in intelligibly picturing to the natural appreciation those stupendous exemplifications of Divine Power, Triumph, and Glory,— those unearthly scenes and wonders which sublime the page of the religious past, and the no less impressive imagery that renders deeply picturesque the religious future.

From these considerations then it is apparent that in becoming possessed of emotions inspired by religious influences, whether of a moral or circumstantial character, we make an effort of imagination, vaster and loftier, than in the reception of any other feeling. In becoming impressed by a religious influence of a circumstantial character we, by exerting our imagination, produce an extended action of our natural appreciation; and in being wrought upon by a religious influence of a moral and comprehensive nature we, by exercising the creative faculty, kindle an extended action of our sympathy. The emotion created in the former circumstances being of such a nature as is produced by the expansion of the mind, and in the latter, by the response of the heart.

Thus, then, it appears that the acquisition of feelings of a religious character involves an exertion of imagination, an extension of appreciation, and an enlargement of sympathy,—by far more considerable than is demanded in the conception of any other order of emotions. We here then arrive at the explanation of that remarkable grandeur and efficiency with which the principle of "Tone and Phrase" rises to the expression of Religious emotions.

For considering that the forms of emotional influence which all circumstances and truths of a lofty and comprehensive character assume, are almost totally sustained in existence by a primary expanse, and subtle glow, of imagination, and thus by an *extended* action of the appreciation and of the sympathy,—that, therefore, the conveyance of such forms of influence—the emotions they inspire, depends almost entirely upon the communication of this internal temper. Considering that the more the existence of any emotional influence depends upon a remarkable vividness and fulness of imagination, and upon a considerable tension of the appreciation and sympathy, the farther will it be understood to lie without the range of the ordinary experience of humanity — the more morally strange and impalpable will it be — the less will it admit of becoming compassed by any of the mediums of *suggestion* that are current amongst mankind; consequently the less must it be such an influence as is calculated to be realised before others by means of the principle of representation, and therefore the less must the imparting of emotions inspired by it lie within the function of the principle of *representation,* and the more must their conveyance fall to the capacity of the principle of *direct communication.* Considering that circumstances and truths of a Religious character are, beyond all others, lofty and comprehensive,—that they involve n being realised, a glow of imagination more vivid and immense than that attending the birth of any other order of feelings,—a glow of imagination grand, unearthly, supernatural, and soaring beyond the confines of this physical universe. Considering that the *flight of appreciation* demanded in the conception of religious feelings is of the loftiest that can be borne by the wings of the human mind, and the *swell of sympathy* the most extended and intense that can rebound from the human heart. Considering that it is the special characteristic of the principle of " Tone and Phrase" to convey the, by other means, wholly inexpressible glow of imagination and spiritual enthusiasm above described, and its peculiar and mysterious property to impart emotions by *direct communication* (of which process the kindling of imagination is the sole visible portion). Considering these things, — is it not at once apparent how completely, in accordance with universal consistency, natural propriety, and with the whole strain of argument advanced in this inquiry,—emotions of a religious character, fall for expression, beyond all others, into the province of the principle of Tone and Phrase.

Considering that the emotions in question fall for expression more undividedly within the province of this great principle than of all others, can we wonder that in their utterance, in development of the resources of its nature, tempered and enhanced by the amassed taste and ingenuity of man, and guided by the mystic inspiration of genius,—it rises—sublimely rises—to its highest and grandest exemplifications? Considering that these exemplifications are in their nature the most advanced manifestations of that principle peculiarly constituted by the Creator for forming the medium for expressing and conveying emotions amongst men — of that principle particularly selected by him to be the etherial language of the feelings of humanity; and ultimately considering the totally chastened and sublime nature of religious emotions—their purity, strength, earnestness, fervour, warmth, constancy, and ever augmenting intensity,—can we wonder that in their expression we meet with such an unearthly and impressive grandeur? Can we fail to account in their utterance by the lofty voice of Music, for a beauty, solemnity, pathos, and power, that is beyond Nature, and which stands apart, in its Divine altitude, from all other effects of Art.

It has been shown, then, in the course of this inquiry, that simple language, eloquence, oratory, Poetry, and Music, are all linked together, and pervaded, by one subtle and pure principle, which conducts throughout the whole course of these demonstrative mediums the emotional current of humanity.

It has been shown that the principal processes by which emotions are conveyed are those of Association, Representation, and Direct communication; and that in these processes the function fulfilled by the subtle principle in question is, in that of *representation*, which embraces all forms of language,—to further and *assist* the reproduction, in its original aspect, of the first incitement of feeling; and in the process of *direct communication*, which constitutes Musical effect,—to be *itself* the sole and direct medium of expression. Into the process of Association the principle in question, in any important capacity, does not enter at all; impressions aroused by association being simply *old impressions*, the resuscitation of which is owing to a stirring of the memory.

The most interesting and striking of these processes, in an artistic, if not in a philosophical sense, is that of *direct communication*. The assumption by an emotion of a *third form* of manifestation, alike distinct from its original external cause, and from the effect of its own existence on the consciousness of its possessor. A *transition state* of feeling; an impalpable influence; distinct from all natural, reproduced, or remembered effects; original, evanescent; equally new and strange to the awakener, as to the contemplator; yet, nevertheless, of itself alone, mysteriously conveying the fine emotion, "the bodiless thought,"— conceived in complexity and conditionally, and imparted in simplicity and unfettered save by the silken streaks of Melody.

Yet, in this ethereal flight, engarbed in such infinite beauty, as befits the spirit-form of emotion. And giving grateful earnest to man, in the high effect of "Music," of that more surpassing loveliness, that still untold charm, that still veiled beauty,—in which he will meet arrayed, the pure thought, the righteous feeling, and the infinite emotion, when "the mind shall be all free."

THE LAWS OF LIFE IN ART.

WRITERS UPON ART MUST IN SOME DEGREE BE ACTORS IN ART.
—THE INTENTION OF THE ORATORIO DEFINED.—NATURE
HERSELF ILLUSTRATES ALL THE ARTS BUT THAT OF MUSIC.
—OF MUSIC SHE CONFERS BUT THE GERMS.—THE GENERAL
LAWS GOVERNING THE EFFECT OF VOCAL (SOLO AND CHORAL),
IN COMPARISON WITH INSTRUMENTAL, MUSIC CONSIDERED.—
THE RESOURCES OF VOCAL MUSIC ARE IN A GREATER DE-
GREE LIMITED BY NATURE THAN THOSE OF INSTRUMENTAL
MUSIC; FOR THIS REASON THE LATTER IS MORE LIABLE TO
ATTAIN AN OVERWROUGHT CONDITION THAN THE FORMER.—
THE MIND ATTACHES TO ITSELF THE RESULTS OF PREVIOUS
MINDS AS PRIMARY DATA FOR ITS OWN OPERATIONS.—A
HISTORY OF THE PURE EFFECTS OF ART A DESIDERATUM.—
THERE IS A TENDENCY IN THE HUMAN MIND IN UNFOLDING
ART TO REJECT THE NATURAL PROMPTINGS OF TASTE, AND
IN THEIR STEAD, TO ACCEPT THE LAWS OF A SYSTEM COM-
PILED BY ITSELF, A SYSTEM WHICH WOULD FAIN GRASP
THE MYSTERIES OF ART EFFECT.—THIS ACCOUNTS FOR MUCH
OF THE DISFIGUREMENT ATTENDING ANCIENT MUSICAL ART, AS
WELL AS MODERN.—THE GENERAL ORDER OF PROGRESS IN
ART POURTRAYED.—THE MIND (THE GENERAL HUMAN MIND),
LIKE THE BODY, DEMANDS NOURISHMENT OF INCREASED IN-
TENSITY AS ITS AGE ADVANCES.—THIS TENDENCY TO BE RE-
STRAINED WITHIN BOUNDS, OR ART MUST BECOME UNINTELLI-
GIBLE; AS THE FORM OF ART APPEALS TO THE SENSES, AND
THESE CAN ONLY GRASP EFFECTS OF WHICH THE COMPLEXITY
IS LIMITED.—THE SPIRIT, NOT THE FORM OF ART MAY BE
ENDLESSLY VARIED.—DICTATES OF ACTION DEDUCED.

III.

THE LAWS OF LIFE IN ART.

IN regarding comprehensively and deeply the whole field of Art; in eliminating certain prevailing truths from its general aspect, one primary condition presents itself, — that the point of view be within the sphere of contemplation.

It must have become matter of observation that all authoritative writers who, in the contemplation of Art, have gathered truths of general interest and edification, have only attained this copious survey of artistic effect, through their more intimate sympathy with one of its tributary streams.

For the field of Art, with regard to moral explorers, appears to enjoy a special immunity distinguishing it from all other areas of human effort. Over its walks not even the generalizing historian or the passionless moralist can unchallenged pass. The latent truth and beauty of that page only reveals itself to minds attuned to the theme through the perfect consciousness of a subordinate knowledge. It is a Kingdom inaccessible to solitary reason; only open to faith, and one which ere it becomes realized demands in its votaries the light of a previous revelation.

In these pages the few general art-truths revealed, are arrived at through considerations starting from the *musical* form of Art, as other important and prevailing truths have been discovered by writers whose main path of exploration has been the art of Painting.

The points of interest in the progress of Art generally to be unfolded in the ensuing observations, will be led to by considering in the first place that high form of Musical composition, "Oratorio."

The artistic intention of a Sacred Oratorio is a grand, comprehensive, and replete expression of that momentous phenomenon of the human heart, religious emotion; the lofty utterance of this expression being, by the law of natural propriety and universal consistency, rendered possible to no other voice in the possession of mankind except that of music—the culmination of the effects of the principle of tone and phrase—the language of the feelings of humanity. Painting, as has been elsewhere remarked, being able to express but so much of religious emotion as can visibly appear in the aspect of the human countenance; and language being only able to indicate the existence of devotional feeling in its outward action upon things. Its inward action upon the human heart —the deep rapture of spirit and sublimity of nature attending its possession, still remaining uninvoked from their silent intensity in the breast of man.

But it is not presumed that even music, with its great resources of impression, and its vast power of emotional utterance, is fully equal to the awful expression of religious emotion in its internal influence upon the human heart, and in the solemn glory of nature attending its possession. For nature, in determining how far those resources for man's indulgence that are not directly available for his practical service, shall be fairly admitted into her human economy, seems, whilst implying the *possession* of emotion, the most serious and important of her great arrangements; to pronounce, a medium appropriate for its entire and direct communication, a luxury for man so ethereal and transcendent as to be inconsistent with the present conditions of his existence.

Thus, whilst Nature herself has developed to an extent far beyond what the mind of man could ever have conceived, the principle of Painting, she has introduced into her great plan only the *germs* of the principle of Music; whilst she herself completely *illustrates* the principles of nearly all the other arts; of music she gives but the principles alone, leaving their exemplification to man. Whilst the bright boundless picture gallery of the Great Painter may be entered whilst treading the ordinary, practical path of life; the temple of Music can *only* be gained by stepping a little aside to the shady groves of elevated leisure.

And it is here alone where we can listen to that mysterious voice whose sound has been denied us amidst the general murmur of life—the voice of human feeling. It is here alone where the great emotional undercurrent of the world breaks forth into visible streams. It is here alone where that indelible and momentous cypher, graved by passion upon the heart of man, bursts into burning charracters of flame.

Such are the conditions of its existence amongst us, of that influence whose high property it is to bestow a form upon, and render apparent to, the senses of man, that otherwise shapeless and voiceless phenomena of the inner world—human emotion. But if it were otherwise; if in addition to the bestowment upon mankind of full facility for the intercommunication of facts; nature had developed amidst us a medium available for the complete expression of human feeling. If amidst the allotment of other resources for man's indulgence, there had been included the elevated and chastened resource of being able to fully impart to others the feelings of the heart—the silent sympathy—the voiceless love—the noiseless rapture—the rayless glory. What harmonies would flow! What songs would rise! What varied eloquence would stir the air of daily life! What a mighty symphony, burthened with pathos and prayer, would ascend from humanity to the intent ears of Heaven!

Nevertheless, there has still been bestowed upon us the elements of this momentous tongue, the germs of this heavenly influence; which man, by his great gift of intellect, and enlightened by God through the almost preternatural inspiration of genius, hath developed into an effect of not small impressive power, and with a voice of emotional utterance soaring beyond Nature and rising loudly in its mighty power into the remote realms of Art. Realms which become solemn as they near that elevation where art becomes truth,—the truth of the spiritual world.

Turning our attention to the form assumed by the order of composition termed "Oratorio" in its material frame, we find that this is highly consistent with its moral intention. We find that the "subject matter" of this work of art is a comprehensive episode from the page of human life, in which all the species and variations of worldly influences that affect the body or soul of man are naturally and faithfully represented; and if we consider the nature of those epochs of human history, from which this episode is selected—epochs in which it was habitual to consider the most ordinary as well as the most special circumstances of life—the most trivial as well as the most serious occurrences—the smallest as well as the most miraculous deliverances—the most insignificant as well as the most overwhelming afflictions—as under the direct regulation of the Almighty; when it was habitual to appeal to him in all things, great or small; to regard all worldly occurrences in what we should now term a *religious light;* in fact, when it was habitual to practically and *externally* acknowledge that relationship of God to humanity which is now mostly *inwardly understood;*—if we consider these circumstances, we are more than ever impressed with the fitness and appropriateness of these incidents and conditions of humanity for representing those circumstances, amidst which the great tide of man's feeling towards God and his brother man would mostly arise.

In the next place, turning our attention to that combination which the material resources of Music assume in the species of artistic effort in question, we again meet with a remarkable appropriateness and consistency. We here find that the most prominent of these resources are the grand vocal and choral presentations of Music. The peculiar propriety above alluded to is perceived in the consideration that these species of musical effect are developed directly and immediately from the only positive and true indications of the principle of music in Nature, namely, from the principle of "Tone and Phrase" apparent in ordinary human speech. A principle, imperfectly developed as it is by Nature, to which we nevertheless owe all that we still possess of that power of imbuing feeling which is exercised independently of representation, description, or association. A principle to which we owe all of that power of emotional eloquence which is *couched amidst words* though it is not *of them*.

At this period of our reflections it is almost impossible to forbear to recognise the considerations, of both weight and interest, bearing testimony to the remarkable chasteness, earnestness, and dignity of the choral form of Music. For this great effect of Fine Art is one which, possessing the attributes of deep physical and moral impressiveness, still derives, of all other effects of art, the least assistance from the physical influences of nature, and yet contains a greater proportion of her spiritual ones. It is an effect from which the influence of matter is wholly excluded; the elements of its existence being a tone of sentiment, a latent action of intellect, and that effect of nature the most uncorporeal, ethereal — and of all the outward indications of emotion that we are conscious of, that one most closely and immediately connected with emotion itself,—the human voice.

Here is suggested that consideration which betrays the remarkable dignity and earnestness of the choral species of musical effect. For if this effect of art is a legitimate development of those principles of nature indicated by the accent and fall, emphasis and pause, tone and phrase, in human speech. And if, as can most assuredly be observed, the moral function and practical property of these principles is to impart, as far as nature's imperfect development of them will permit, — human emotion, independently of representation, description, or association, and by means *of direct communication*. If, in truth, they are the elements of that momentous, deep-burthened, and Heaven-withheld language of human emotion, that in some great day must burst into life with supernatural emphasis and heavenly cadence; and by which the general heart of humanity will be relieved and understood. How, in an argumentative sense, awful in its dignity; how solemn in its earnestness; how elevated in character, and worthy of man's highest respect, must be that humble but nearest earthly approach to its mighty eloquence which has, in the effect of choral enunciation, been achieved by man, through a chaste and legitimate development of those of its principles betrayed,—in the emphasis and pause, tone and phrase of human speech—by Nature!

But there is another attribute which the species of music under consideration possesses, besides the attribute of earnestness—dignity, and that of inspiring respect. For choral expression being, as I have before observed, that species of æsthetical effect where there is the least of art, except in its most spiritual sense; where there is most of the unembodied beauty of nature; is, in consistency with these circumstances, the least liable to attain that overwrought condition of corrupted splendour and emblazoned decay to which all arts with elements less purely natural are extremely liable; and the most tenacious in preserving that chastity of original outline, that unalterable and only true embodiment of its first intention, which we see always unsulliedly retained in the works of nature.

In this respect, not only does the effect of art in question betray a distinctive contrast in comparison to other orders of æsthetical effect, but also to other species of that order of influence to which it itself belongs. This contrast being visible betwixt choral and instrumental music, and the consideration of this contrast will, I hope, lead us to the perception of a great and comprehensive moral in the human ministration of Art generally.

The very limitation of the resourses of choral music is an exemplification of that deep *restrictive* principle in nature, which is the soul of all true liberty and lofty elevation; it is the *bondage* of religion which *frees* and upraises the soul. In the same way the very freedom and vague scope of the resources of instrumental music is an example of that dangerous latitude which leads to oblivion.

Thus we perceive the reason why choral music, though restricted in its mechanical resources, is still boundless, infinite, and unsurpassably sublime in its powers of moral impressiveness.

Although the vague scope of instrumental, in comparison with the limited resources of choral, music has been spoken of as an example of a dangerous latitude; in the instrumental form, the principle of restriction still exists, though not so definitely perceivable as in the choral order of musical effect. The distinction between the circumstances of its existence in the one species of music, and the other, betrays itself in the consideration that the latter form of musical effect being that in which, as has been previously explained, the principles of nature are *the least alloyed by artificial interference*, it must therefore betray more conspicuously, forcibly, and indelibly, that principle of restriction to constitutional form and original chastity of outline which nature steadfastly and unequivocally observes in all her developments of the principle of beauty. Whilst the former species of musical effect being an influence in which the development of the principle of beauty is left to man, it is left to him also to discover *where the true position of the principle of restriction lies*; where, in fact, the true path to æsthetical effect may be lost, and thus that great ascent indubiously found.

Now it is in this consideration where the moral of these arguments is approached. Where, amidst the ample development of beauty in its human ministration, shall we determine is the great line of restriction drawn by natural propriety and universal consistency.

The true boundaries of the path to æsthetical effect, prescribed by the hidden conditions with which nature has endowed it, if they are not felt by the subtle and ethereal standard of taste in the breast of man, the *conscience* of the artistic being, can only be demonstrated (like the boundaries of the path of morality to those who have not the inscrutable internal testator of good and evil) by a reference to the page of history, and with the illustration of nature.

In reviewing the history of Art, the chronicle of the dispensation of beauty by man, we are in the first place impressed with the remarkable fact that many effects, which we are accustomed to regard as the *primary* æsthetical data originally conferred by nature, are in truth not so; but, on the other hand, a considerable *development* of that data by man—a development occupying a considerable portion of the path of Art.

It is remarkable with what unconscious regularity and assiduity, the mind takes hold of the conclusions of other minds, and of the effects of art wrought out in a long strain of preceding mental effort, and attaches the same to itself as abstract materials for the construction of fresh truths, as primary æsthetical data belonging to nature, and by her directly conferred for the human operations of taste and for the developments of art.

The consideration of this truth shews us how necessary is a knowledge of the history of the pure effects of art in perceiving the true relationship of artistic works. For though their abstract superiority may be visible by solely direct contemplation, still it is only in the above circumstances from whence can be obtained the view of their relative superiority, their real merit, and the true greatness of their conceivers.*

* A history to my knowledge yet unwritten. It, however, involves a most fertile field of exertion, and, when duly accomplished, would constitute the most perfect, complete, and the grandest theory of the musical art extant. For the great composers are in truth, the best theorists. They deduce the laws and arrange the materials of musical effect from the inscrutable instinct of taste implanted in the breast of Genius, and a systematic arrangement of musical effects in the order in which they sprung from the minds of these would be the true and only system of musical development. The old theorists grope about the effects of Music to discover the laws and construction of those effects, as an artist might pick a flower to pieces in order to unravel the mysteries of its æsthetic influence. Certainly they discover laws, but the laws of the theorists are not by far of general application, and only adapt them-

But if from the history of Art, we discover (when the stream is fairly in motion) a strong tendency in the mind to attach to itself human wrought effects selves exactly to the simplest of musical effects. They are swept remorselessly over as every fresh development of the musical art takes place. What havoc have not Beethoven and Mendelssohn made with the old rules relating to the progression and construction of chords, and to the principles of modulation! Not but to the great, earnest, and learned musical analysts an infinite debt is owed by all subsequent musicians. The stern limit by which they circumscribed the means of musical effect has had the result of causing the primitive resources of this effect to be well and thoroughly probed and explored. It has also stimulated immensely the constructive tendencies of the human mind, and nursed into vigour the germs of creative idea which might otherwise have become scattered and lost in the endless diversions of the fancy. It has kept the field of Music pure from the weeds of meretricious effect and, bestowed upon the Art certain lasting forms. At the same time it must be still remembered, that the old theoretical laws with regard to the present state of the musical art, involve exceptions nearly as often as they apply, and that the grammar from whence they issue does not by far, embrace all the resources of this great Art—language. There is at least room for enlarging in this department of musical resource, and the history of musical effects above alluded to—that is, of those striking and unique combinations and progressions, which, though originally, incidentally conceived and specially applied, have now become common constructional material—connecting conventionalities in general musical expression,—a history of these would, in my opinion, be the best mode of bringing up the march of musical analysis to the present state of the Art.

of art as data conferred by nature; from the same page, in remarkable contrast, do we also discover (in the true infancy of art, when all data is by far more contracted, and when what exists of it is solely constituted by that conferred by nature) a similarly strong tendency of the human mind to *ignore* this natural data, and to endeavour to replace it by a hopeless search after those ethereal principles of art upon which all its effects depend, but which are ever hidden.

This latter tendency of the human mind is illustrated by, and at the same time explains, that period of the development of musical art when musical effect was endeavoured to be deduced from abstruse calculations of the mind, instead of from the governed impulses of the breast.

But the grand discovery to be drawn from a contemplation of the glowing page of art, is the solution of the problem—where are the *true boundaries* of the great human ascent to æsthetical splendour?

Glancing comprehensively upon the history of that beauty which is ministered by man, upon the path in which all art has trod, both that which has declined and fallen, and that which is still in life and vigour; what prevailing order of progress do we see?

We see the first developments of beauty moulded

by man possess a definiteness of character approaching to starkness; a unity of design that borders upon poverty, a decision of outline approaching to asperity, and a positiveness of form that verges to ungracefulness.

But as the spring of beauty dawns more fully within the soul of man, behold the lines of art, the symbols of the spirit of beauty, flow more gracefully; the artistic idea is revealed more softly; its aspect becomes warmer, and teems with lofty expression; whilst it still betrays a *definiteness* of form, *decision* of character, *unity* of design and *purity* of outline.

Again, as the summer of art approaches, all the softer and warmer characters of beauty that glow in the artistic idea, become more intense, and *bud into ornament*. Its expression beams in ineffable loveliness and lofty grace, whilst its effect is considerably augmented and rendered massive by the partially extraneous but still legitimate resources of the mind.

This is the culmination of artistic life.

But, anon, the teaming floriture of ornament flows so profusely, so enrichingly, but, at the same time, so enervatingly over the gorgeous form of art, that the transcendent lines of pure beauty become defiled and broken. Whilst simultaneously the infinite resources of the mind for artificially developing,—for apparently increasing, by mechanical reflections,—original sparks of beauty; become so extensively exemplified in the now changing aspect of art, that that simple but unsurpassable eloquence of native beauty—the impressive and plainly graved lore from the human soul in its elevated temperament—is totally concealed or altogether extinct. And the lofty missioned expression of art now wholly teems with dazzling, soulless ornament (the abused exemplification of that abstract principle of outward charm which nature has enjoined shall always more or less vividly, and everywhere consistently, shine in all operations in the universe, mental or physical), or creeps weakly upon the mind, bearing only the multiplied echoes of original beauty—the fading reflections of her first spark; though the din of artificial resource strikes loudly upon the ear, and the glare of mechanical display dazzles and distracts the eye.

About here, then, is the line where the path of human art verges upon diffuseness, confusion, and, in fact, death and oblivion. Here is the spot where the spoiled but heavenly child of humanity is tottering upon the brow of darkness. Where the year bending, loaded with gorgeous array, is sinking into the wintry obscure. Here is the spot where the bright trace of the spirit of Beauty upon earth becomes straggling and indefinite; where she may assuredly become lost; where the track of her sweet footsteps may for ever disappear to the beaming eye of man.

Therefore here doth it behove the human ministers of Beauty, the earthly shepherds of Art, to glance back and attentively contemplate, the clearer and purer outlines displayed in the path of her more youthful footsteps.

The cause of this apparent inevitable tendency of Art to flourish from simplicity to graceful and replete variety; from this to inordinate splendour, and then to be caught in the rapid current of corruption;—to advance like all things on earth from youth to prime, and thence into the mist of age; lies in the hidden constitution of the human mind, formed in its action for the admission of that inscrutable element common to almost every work, act, or motive, that proceeds from man; the element of fallibility.

For the general outline of the human mind, extending throughout generations, and in its long and unbroken path of life involving the rise and fall of thousands of the mortal shrines in which it temporarily dwells, may be still at length observed to betray the same general features of its career as is so distinctly revealed in that of its earthly abodes.

Thus, in that exhibition of the nature of the mind revealed in its action upon Art, we see it demands, like the body, nourishment of continually increased intensity, as its age advances. Then, when its form is developed, still, like the body, we see it betray that proneness to reject the natural food of health, and demand excitement in an ever-augmented degree. For owing to the remarkable property of the human mind, previously mentioned—of unconsciously attaching to itself, as innate data of operation, the results amassed in the preceding portion of its life,—it will be seen that, as every fresh intellect arises upon the scene of Art, the nourishment which satisfied the previous one has already become constituent operative data of the new one, which consequently, in obedience to the ennobling principle of restlessness in its nature, demands fresh and original forms of manifestation; till that limit which circumscribes every series of influences appealing to the outward senses—and the *form* of art is one of these—is arrived at; till the confines previously mentioned are reached, where the mind, if it alter its *outward form of manifestation*, must repeat; or where its tendency for change may cause it to diverge into the regions of excitement and oblivion.

Is not, then, the path of Art endless? Is it not ever and ever varied? Is it not inexhaustible? No! unless it be the endlessness of the circle. The depth of Beauty revealed by the medium of Art is unfathomable—can never by far be wholly received into the expansive mind of man. But the *forms of its revelation* upon earth can only succeed each other, can only move, in a cycle; like the rain that falls from heaven, is the same that fell before; like the flower of the field, which betrays first the germ, then the stem; the leaf, the bud, the blossom, and the flower. For *further effect* than any of these it must ever drink the rain, and smile to the sun in vain.

These facts are illustrated by, and at the same time explain, the present condition of the arts of Poetry and Music, now at the termination of their cycle, in which ornament and floriture teem in formless and boundless exuberance; in which an abandoned array of gorgeous and sensual imagery, unsubjective to any *definite idea* of beauty, is only lost in the desultory and totally empty mysticism of a wandering and powerless mind; or in the dazzling display of overwrought artificial mechanical resource.

I say again, the depth of the stream of Beauty is fathomless and inexhaustible, and can never be wholly imbibed by the panting soul of man. But its surface,—the page of its earthly revelation,—is definite, compassable, and *circumscribed*. The emotions of the breast of man — extraneously derived — cannot but be received through the medium of the sense; and the number of impressions producible thereon belong to the orders of a finite system. Therefore Art must be repeatitive in form—must flow in a cycle; though the beauty shining from its depths is immortal and infinite. Let then its votaries and exponents relieve their thirst for change in the fathomless depths of Beauty; that infinite spring of ever original idea; and not vainly endeavour to gain from the finite the attributes of the infinite; not seek in the mortal *form* of Art for that endless progression—for the betrayal of that infinite series of changes, which alone dwells in its immortal *spirit*.

The object of these remarks is to impress how considerably the true progress of Art may be assisted and maintained by an intelligent retrospect of its past course, and by a consideration of that form of its development termed choral, in which its real and only path is more arbitrarily dictated by Nature.

From these considerations we learn that purity

of outline is the specific attribute of true Art; and that simplicity, not complexity, is the soul of deep impression and great effect. That simplicity, far from involving the attribute of shallowness, is the great result of that deep complexity which divine intellect alone can organise or follow; complexity whose effect alone is revealed to man in those instincts peculiar to genius, and which genius alone can wield—the instincts of simplicity.

We learn also that as that darkness and want of warmth which surrounds *the dawn of Art* proceeds from the tendency of the human mind to ignore the æsthetical data proffered by nature—the only medium through which man can hold communion with the hidden spirit of Beauty—the only agency through which he can avail himself of her principles; that so also that darkness which hovers around the *decline of Art* proceeds from a similar tendency, namely, *to reject the agency of nature;* to reject those legitimate artistic forms, which, although in their construction they have involved the exertions of generations of intellect; still through the very closeness of their relationship with the human mind, through the tendency it betrays to avail itself of them as its most natural and effective forms of manifestatation, may be termed the simple forms of Nature.

We learn that as that harshness and confusion,

which disfigures the infancy of Art, proceeds from an endeavour of the human mind to supply the loss of the data proffered by Nature—of Nature's illustrations of the principles of beauty, the nearest rudiments of her system open to the study of man, —by substituting effects from a *complete system of beauty compiled by himself;* (an abortive system imagined by him to be that on which Nature's charm—which he has thus relieved of its sacred and eternal mystery — is wrought;) that so also the harshness and confusion disfiguring Art at the period of its decline, proceeds from a similar vain presumptuous endeavour in the mind *to supersede Nature*; to substitute for that deep and only type of true grandeur and sublimity, that sole embodiment of finished complexity — complexity that arrives at a result—that weaves itself into the mystery of the sublime, namely, Simplicity—an impotent and distracting complexity of the mind of man. To supply by *artificial, mechanical, and overwrought resource,* those effects and impressions which alone can be wrought by an *impulse of the breast;* an impulse kindled by a communion with the spirit of Beauty, and arrayed in the legitimate resources of Art, but still a simple and single impulse of nature, as exemplified in the history of Art and in the works of genius.

We learn that although in contrast to the early action of the human mind, with regard to Art, the intermediate development of her form to its prime was wrought through the tendency of the mind to attach to itself all the previous effects of art as data for new ones;—that still the impetus the mind thus received for continual enhancement and enlargement of Form in Art, led it to forget her Spirit—the spirit of Beauty for whose revelation it is alone that Art exists—and eventually to outstrip the Form.

And thus we arrive at the perception of dictates of action with regard to Art which are obvious and imperative—(and the subject is one of no superficial or unpractical character, for that which is Beauty to the mind may be considered to have been ordained by the Creator as the great symbol and illustration of Virtue to the heart), namely—to return to and abide zealously and scrupulously in, that highly developed form of Art which is still consistent with Nature; lest, by endeavouring to substitute for the simplicity and intelligibility arrived at in Nature, and developed by Art in her replete and legitimate Forms, an artificial complexity of the mind of Man; by endeavouring to produce by overwrought *mechanical resource*, that great impression of Beauty and Sublimity which can alone be imparted by a *legitimately arrayed impulse of the breast*—which is alone visible through the long-tried path, beaten by the previous and continued march of the human mind — we lose altogether a glimpse of its brightness; and rashly drive on effects of sense—as though, in variety and power, they could surpass their finite nature —till we gain a velocity which has the effect of stillness; a light which intensifies to darkness, and a complexity not to be distinguished from confusion.

For EU product safety concerns, contact us at Calle de José Abascal, 56–1°,
28003 Madrid, Spain or eugpsr@cambridge.org.

www.ingramcontent.com/pod-product-compliance
Ingram Content Group UK Ltd.
Pitfield, Milton Keynes, MK11 3LW, UK
UKHW040158230326
469255UK00012B/159